Fire & Ice

Fire & Ice

THE HISTORY OF
THE SAINT PAUL
WINTER CARNIVAL

Moira F. Harris

ISBN 1-880654-28-8

Library of Congress Catalogue Card No. 2002-114284

Produced by Stanton Publication Services, Inc.,
with page layout and design by Ann Elliot Artz.

Cover design by Mighty Media.

Front cover design based on photograph courtesy of the
St. Paul Festival and Heritage Foundation, and
rear cover float drawings courtesy of Steve Shumaker.

Except where noted, all illustrations are courtesy of the
Saint Paul Festival and Heritage Foundation.

Printed in Canada

Contents

Preface

By Gareth Hiebert, "Oliver Towne" columnist for the St. Paul Pioneer Press

I wasn't around for the first Saint Paul Winter Carnival in 1886, but I didn't miss many from 1940 to 1975, starting with the World War II era.

That year, 1940 – was a patriotic parade of bands, men and women in uniform, their marching units in vivid, heavy wool costumes – all competing for Home Front cheers.

Return of the "heroes" was celebrated with the zaniest parade ever assembled. It was held in February of 1946 – rather late – to give the boys time to get home. It began on Summit Avenue near the University Club and thousands of veterans wound in weird, out-of-step ranks, through the downtown. Crowds lined the route, cheering their loved ones and often running out to offer bottles of beer and more so that the finish was a little unsteady.

Frank Madden, the mayor's secretary, penned the Legend of Boreas and now we had the plot of regal King Boreas challenged by wily "womanizer" Vulcanus Rex and his henchmen. Now the women of the city were prey to kissings and smooching with black grease pens. And hundreds of women lined up for kisses or went into hiding.

I savored roles in both camps – in the Vulcan Krewe of 1959 and as Prime Minister in 1962. Playing both parts was like army basic training.

John Geisler came to the Winter Carnival as its new director in the early 1950s and proceeded to turn a regional celebration into a nationwide extravaganza. Geisler and his publicist, Dave Speer, brought exciting new life to the Carnival, including Ed Sullivan, Steve Allen, the "Queen for a Day" show, Mitzi Gaynor, and Carol Channing. Dinah Shore rode a toboggan down the Cedar street obstacle course.

Geisler recruited acts and winter celebrations from cities and towns across Minnesota. He brought kings and queens and princesses to the Carnival until the St. Paul Hotel looked like a palace of beauties. He also brought many thousands of visitors, who brought their money.

In 1958 Rohland Thomssen, the first King Boreas from America ever to travel to Europe, and his wife, were invited to the Brussels World's Fair with side trips to Germany, Austria, and Scandinavia. Rolly rode off the airplane in Munich on a bicycle, in his uniform. Then he began to hand out his souvenir gold coins. The Germans rushed to get them but, alas, they were only valuable in the Realm of Boreas.

With the Hamm's Brewery for support, the Carnival went to the Seattle World's Fair, the New York World's Fair, and three Rose Bowls. Its floats always won blue ribbons.

We brought the entire royal party to the New York World's Fair and were greeted by actor Pat O'Brien and singer Carmel Quinn.

We rode in the Tournament of Roses Parade of 1963 and spent five hours on the float, which might have strained our kidneys, except that spectators along the way were used to this dilemma and invited us to use their facilities.

Our host at the Tournament was a vice-president of the Bank of America. He told me that the year before, when Minnesota played in the Rose Bowl, he had gotten an autographed football for a lad living in Bayport who had polio. When I got home I checked and met Johnny St. Marie, a high school senior with a severe polio handicap. He had the football as a prized possession. I wrote about him and my story was parlayed into a VFW scholarship that helped put him through law school.

My King Boreas, Bud Chandler, who made burial vaults, always got the biggest ovations in small town festivals from the employees of funeral homes.

It was like CAMELOT for almost forty years, people always said. The king was Boreas and his queen was Guinevere, the Queen of Snows. They were surrounded by the Princes and Princesses of the winds. There were ice palaces, parades, and sporting events.

It was a wonderful time I remember.

Introduction & Acknowledgments

Everybody who has spent a winter in St. Paul probably knows a little about the Winter Carnival. The parades, the Ice Palace, the races and the competitions, and visiting celebrities, all become part of the experience of living here. Buttons, photographs, and many other souvenirs help recreate these memories.

The St. Paul Winter Carnival is not only Minnesota's oldest civic celebration, but one of the oldest in the nation. Events and programs launched in St. Paul would inspire other cities to hold their own winter festivals just as Montreal's Carnival influenced St. Paul. Other Minnesota communities would begin festivals as unique in their own way as the Winter Carnival. For example, there is Minneapolis' Aquatennial and the Heart of the Beast May Day parades, the Anoka Halloween parade, and in St. Paul, Cinco de Mayo and Grand Old Days.

For some, as I have learned, the Winter Carnival becomes a lifetime involvement. Louis W. Hill, Sr., was a member of a toboggan club in 1886, president of the Carnival organization in 1916 and 1917, and a member of the revival organization group in 1937. Strengthened by family ties more than one generation may take part in Carnival pageantry and events. Tim Madden, Boreas Rex LXVI (2002), is the grandson of the third Boreas Rex, 1937's Frank Madden. Fathers and sons enlist in Boreas' family or Vulcan's ranks as they come to appreciate the camaraderie developed. Some alternate between portraying the legend characters and taking on administrative assignments. Henry J. Lund handled public relations for the 1930 Midway Carnival and served as Executive Director for the Winter Carnival. His son, William, became Vulcan Rex in 1953.

Women are certainly a major support of Carnival committees, yet so far only one family, an aunt and her niece, can boast of wearing the Queen of the Snows tiara: Dorothy Arneberg (1955) and her niece Margaret Arneberg in 1980. One family counts a Boreas (Victor Reim), a Prime Minister (his daughter, Ann), and years of committee work by both Victor Reim and his wife, Bonnie. They received the Sal LoBaido award for their volunteer services.

For many others the Carnival offers a full schedule of winter events to watch from a sidewalk, an auditorium seat, or a snowy field. Every year has something new and something renewed.

"I most strenuously object to the flagrant desecration of Sunday in the staging of sport events such as the skating contest for boys and others at Lake Como. This sort of desecration reflects no credit on St. Paul and interferes exceedingly with our business as ministers and churches. We look to you to see that this matter of such deep concern to every God-fearing citizen of the city is at once discontinued."

~ George Mahlon Miller, Pastor, Olivet
Congregational Church (January 26, 1917).

Yet always winter plays its unpredictable self. Will Boreas have a castle, will there be sufficient snow or only a trace? Clearly the city now has enough indoor facilities for ceremonies (often in Landmark Center), a parade could march in the skyways, and other events could take place indoors. Yet, the purpose has always been to plan for and triumph over the cold so moving inside doesn't quite seem right.

I'm not sure which was the first Winter Carnival parade that I watched. It may have been one that our family viewed after spending several months in Pasadena where we stood on a much warmer street corner watching a Tournament of Roses parade go by. We saw other parades in St. Paul and, of course, went to the Ice Palaces. Seeing a magically lighted, glistening palace on the shores of a lake or river is an incredible experience, definitely worth a trip even in −20 degree weather, as it was in 1986.

A watcher and visitor hardly becomes aware of the backstage life of the Carnival. Like every civic event it has a history, each year building upon earlier efforts to entertain, celebrate and change a city. This book seeks to capture that history through the printed and photographic record. It is not a history without problems. Lack of cold weather and snow meant cancellation of carnivals. America's involvement in wars, economic downturns, and simple lack of enthusiasm all caused breaks in carnival history at various dates.

"Needless to state that I felt proud of the real 'King' of the Carnival, Louis W. Hill, as he rode along on his spirited steed. Hill has put St. Paul on the Mountain top and we know from holy Scripture — a city on a mountain cannot be hid."

~ Brother Julius, Christian Brothers,
Cretin High School (January 27, 1917).

There would always be some who opposed celebrating winter. The opinion of James J. Hill, the father of Louis W. Hill, Sr., was once given in response to an appeal for financial support of a winter sports carnival. Hill said:

I might give you $50,000 to spend for a greenhouse in which to grow bananas, but not one cent for an affair that would advertise our winter weather. Your show would make outsiders believe that Minnesota is as cold as Alaska (Collier's, *February 26, 1916, 17*).

Downtown business owners were, at times, opposed to closing streets for parades or flooding them to create skating rinks. In 1916 and 1917 temperance leaders urged the city to make sure that bars closed early during Carnival, and local ministers requested that no Carnival activities take place on Sundays. In the 1880s Carnival planners had observed the "not on Sunday" restriction. An even greater problem for the carnival was its Super Ice Palace in 1992. Built to coincide with Super Bowl XXVI being played in Minneapolis, the Ice Palace was the tallest and most expensive ever built. Its cost far exceeded the budget and the resulting financial turmoil nearly ended the Carnival forever.

The Carnival organization relies on the support of its many volunteers and the local business community. That community has changed, however. Many locally-owned firms have closed their doors or, through mergers, become part of larger corporate entities with headquarters (and loyalties) elsewhere. In 1937 marching units from the Emporium, Golden Rule, Schuneman's and Field-Schlick were part of the parade. All of these department stores are now closed and gone, leaving only the former Dayton's (now, Marshall Field's) to represent that category of business. The Theo. Hamm Brewing Company, Hilex, and the railroads so important to the success of the 1916 and 1917 Carnivals, are examples of firms either gone or merged into other corporations which do not support the Carnival.

Many people with knowledge of Carnival history answered my questions. They include Gareth Hiebert, Johanna Mohwinkel, Dick O'Toole, Dot Bentfield, Bill Godwin, Mary and Dennis Harris, Eugene and Marilyn DiMartino, Bob Edgett, Shirley and Steve Shumaker, Helen and Dick Murphy, John Fisher, Tom Swain, Bob Sheild, Ted Zwieg, Dorothy Furlong, Lonny and Elon Piche, John Meyers, Steve Popovich, Bob Olsen, Sandy Schwartzbauer, Robert Viking, Charlie Hall, Tom Keller, Bill LaLonde, Bob Fletcher, Sr., Walt and Lynn Hedblum, Joan Norris, Bill Rust, Jean West, Bonnie Reim, Bob Jackson, Karen Vento, Pat Steineman, Eileen McCormack, Shar Salisbury, Bill Wald, Matt and Bobbie Wiederkehr, Curt Wescott, Lorraine Venaas, Doug Wetherby, and Mary Capra, as well as others on the staffs of the Minnesota Historical Society, Ramsey County Historical Society, and the James J. Hill Reference Library. In the pages which follow the archival collections of the Minnesota Historical Society (St. Paul Winter Carnival Association or SPWCA and the St. Paul Outdoor Sports Association or SPOSA), and the James J. Hill Reference Library (Louis W. Hill, Sr., Papers, or "Hill Papers") will be cited frequently. Although Louis W. Hill omitted the dreaded word "Winter" in the name of his Carnivals in 1916 and 1917, for consistency's sake references will be made to the "Winter Carnival" throughout, as that was always when it was held.

Sadly, John Geisler and David Speer, whom many cite as major sources of information, died before I could interview them. They, and other Carnival leaders such as Louis Hill, Sr., and George Thompson, made the Winter Carnival happen. That such is still happening 117 years after its wildly successful inaugural year in 1886 says something about what their creation has meant to the city, the state, and to our attitude towards winter.

Moira F. Harris
St. Paul, Minnesota
March 15, 2003

The borders of early stereopticon cards were often used for publicity purposes.

An Idyl On Ice

By J. H. Hanson

The Ice King was feverish,
Fretful and sad
In all his long reign
He had ne'er been so bad.
He'd swear at the lackeys
Throw boots at the cat
And insisted on wearing
Last summer's straw hat.

He'd tell an old story, or sing an old song.
But fly in a rage at the Queen's chestnut gong.
He said unkind things with a terrible frown
When the Queen proudly showed him her new winter crown.

So hot grew the blood
Of this great Arctic Caesar,
He was packed to the neck
In a big ice cream freezer.
'Twas detestable weather,
Now cold, and now hot
And the King vowed, old Hazen's
Predictions were rot.

The cold weather flag,
He nailed tight and fast
On the castle's high tower
To a very tall mast.
One day 'twas so cold
That the icebergs all froze,

And the king wore a muff
On his blue blooded nose.
Why, the seals on the shores
Were found shedding tears
For the cold was so great
It had nipped off their ears.

Then again
'Twas so hot
That all wore
Summer suits,
And the King
Sloshed around
In his big
Rubber boots.

The climax was reached for this terrible Nero
When the arctic thermometer climbed up to zero.
His royal nibs sank and seemed past all hope,
His appetite left; he did nothing but mope.
The doctors prescribed their nostrums and pills
But all they could do, only increased his ills.

One day in a hammock,
With his big palm leaf fan
In his shirt sleeves lay stretched
This royal sick man.

By the side of the King
Queen Aurora

Sat rocking
And darning the heel
Of Prince Blizzard's stocking.

The patient who slept 'neath the warm frigid breeze
Awoke with a start, and a tremendous sneeze
"I'll knock them all out in one round, let them time it.
'Taint medicine I want, but a square change of climate.
Their liver pads, tonics, ague pills and thin broth
Won't do for a monarch
Brought up in the north.

"We'll go to Saint Paul
The Queen of the world.
The Ice Monarch's banner
Shall be there unfurled.

"Tis a place
Thricely blessed.
Climate, commerce, condition,
All aid to produce
A great city's Position.

"They're prompt at all calls
And never are careless,
Send them word to build soon
A fine royal palace.

"Call quick Winter Zephyr, Lord Chancellor high
And bid him to let not an hour go by
Before he has issued
A grand proclamation
And sent it abroad
To every known nation
To every name from Alpha to Izzard.
Done here at the palace of ancient White Blizzard."
Now all was commotion, and hurry, and bustle,
The King showed that he was not slow on the rustle
He ate, and he slept, and forgot he was sick,
And bought him a ready made ulster on tick.
He got his own luncheon
And packed his own trunks
And winked his left eye at all the quidnuncs.

At Xmas old Santa Claus
Started ahead,

Instructed to telephone
Back how things stood.

The King sent a load
As high as a steeple
Of beautiful gifts
For his good, loyal people.
The message came back
"Hello. Hurry up.
You're expected first month,
And third Monday to sup."

The now merry King
And his royal court gay,
Set forth for Saint Paul
In gorgeous array.

Their reception was splendid,
A perfect ovation.
Tens of thousands were there
From all the broad nation.

The carnival came,
A festival grand
It never was equalled
In any known land
With processions and pageants
And music and fêtes
For fully two weeks
The joy
Ne'er abates.

Many thousands of men in uniforms bright,
Stood by the old king when called on to fight.
The Fire King, jealous,
Made two fierce assaults
But came out of season
His plans all proved false.
Borealis grew hearty,
Fat, merry, robust
And vowed that forever
In Saint Paul he'd trust.
Instruct now the people, the high and the low
Who seek all good things to Saint Paul to go.
They'll find great prosperity, plenty of wealth,
And as did their King, they're sure to find "Health."

SAINT PAUL

Ice Palace

AND

Winter Carnival

SOUVENIR

The Business of Carnival

1

The concept of the St. Paul Winter Carnival was first discussed at a meeting in the brand new Ryan Hotel on November 2, 1885. Forty or more gentlemen were invited, most of whom were founders or proprietors of St. Paul's principal businesses. George Thompson, publisher of the *St. Paul Dispatch*, is credited with suggesting the Carnival, an idea which was readily accepted. H. J. Fairchild, later to be a member of the Carnival's board of directors, commented that it was "the first proposition of a public nature he ever knew that was not opposed by somebody" (*St. Paul Daily Globe*, November 3, 1885, 4).

The usual reason given for beginning the St. Paul Winter Carnival was that it was a chance to show the country how Minnesotans spent the winter, enjoying outdoor activities in their healthy, bracing climate. Montreal's winter carnival had been financially successful, but an outbreak of smallpox had forced the cancellation of the event for 1886. Thus St. Paul, with only a few short months to do the work, sought to replace Montreal and become North America's "Winter Carnival" city.

In the period after the Civil War business leaders in many cities were intrigued with the idea of fairs or carnivals. The giant world's fairs (Philadelphia in 1876, New Orleans in 1885, Chicago in 1893 and San Francisco in 1894) brought attention, tourism, and income to a city, but these were once-in-a-lifetime events. Annual events, however, although smaller, could be depended upon to reap the publicity and establish a city in the nation's consciousness. In the summer Minnesota already had its State Fair, now ensconced in the Midway district after wandering from venue to venue for a number of years. Minneapolis had its grand Industrial Exposition building (opened in August, 1885), where indoor events and conventions could be held, but there was no competition for a January – February event in the entire state or region.

Businessmen in several Midwestern cities also looked into the idea of holding annual festivals. In Omaha the result was both two world's fairs and the Ak-Sar-Ben festivities. In St. Louis a very

> **"To rent. College Avenue, 24 – Elegant furnished for rent, good view of ice palace; reasonable terms; board next door."**
>
> ~ St. Paul Daily News (January 22, 1888).

> **"More than 5,000 rooms in addition to those listed at the carnival association are needed to take care of the visitors who are coming to the fete."**
>
> ~ St. Paul Daily News (January 14, 1917, 3).

secretive group began the Veiled Prophet parades and balls in 1877. Like the Winter Carnival there was a legend, a mythic history to the Veiled Prophet festival involving camels and a visitor from the East. The Veiled Prophet festivities grew out of a fall harvest festival concept while all World's fairs were summer events. Only St. Paul was willing to confront the vagaries of winter.

> "Then a year ago St. Paul made a discovery. It discovered winter and in so doing found its soul."
> ~ *Albert Britt*, Outing Magazine *(March, 1917).*

The earliest Winter Carnival Souvenir, copyrighted in 1885.

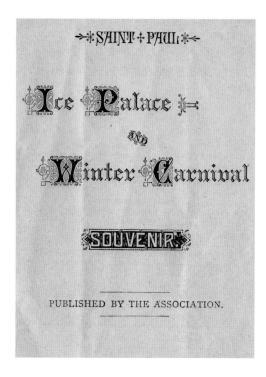

One reason often offered for the birth of the Winter Carnival is the "insult." A newspaper journalist is supposed to have compared St. Paul to Siberia and deemed it uninhabitable in winter. We have been unable to trace the source of this quote, although J. H. Hanson refers to "Hazen's predictions" in his poem. General William Babcock Hazen may have written the words. Hazen had published articles and letters in the 1870s opposing the plans of the Northern Pacific Railroad. A Civil War veteran who had seen years of duty in the Western states, Hazen believed that the railroad was being deceitful and dishonest in promoting investment and immigration to the Northern plains. He argued that both cold weather and a lack of water made agriculture a very risky proposition there and that the available land was far from being the Garden of Eden situation that railroad advertising suggested.

Why the Siberian comparison mattered to nineteenth century Minnesotans relates to immigration and economic development. The Twin Cities (or "duel cities," as one reporter described them) were growing faster than any other communities in the nation. People were coming both to settle and for health reasons, even in winter, as Ralph Brown noted in his *Minnesota History* article. Anyone who suggested that the cold would be uncomfortable or make life hazardous affected plans of business leaders who were busily supporting immigration from Germany and Sweden.

One published comment was that of a *New York Times* reporter who visited Minnesota in 1884 to report on the rivalry between Minneapolis and St. Paul. He was amused that both cities had new, large hotels, the West in Minneapolis and the Ryan (almost completed) in St. Paul. He liked the venison and trout which he tasted, but he did think the weather was cold.

He wrote:

*It is sometimes rather cool in St. Paul and the surrounding country. Everybody wears furs in this latitude. Immense overcoats of bear, wolf and buffalo hide encircle the cabmen, the street car drivers, and the draymen. Richer people clothe themselves in the skins of seal and beaver and this gives a very arctic appearance to the city. In the winter it would be an exceedingly good place to establish a training school for North Pole explorers (*The New York Times, *November 28, 1884, 5).*

Over fifty years later (in 1936) another journalist would write far more disparaging words about St. Paul and this, too, would help justify holding a celebration in response.

The business of the Carnival was first established as a corporation, with shares for sale at ten dollars each. The first officers elected were:

George R. Finch, President
George Thompson, Vice President
W. A. Van Slyke, Vice President
A. S. Tallmadge, Secretary
J. H. Hanson, Assistant Secretary
Albert Scheffer, Treasurer

Finch and Van Slyke were partners in Auerbach & Van Slyke, a wholesale house; Thompson was the publisher of the *St. Paul Dispatch*; Scheffer was an officer of the Bank of Minnesota; and Tallmadge was active in real estate. Sixteen other men were selected to serve as the Board of Directors. It was Hanson who wrote the first version of the Carnival legend in "The Crystal Carnival," found in *The Ice Palace and Winter Carnival Souvenir* (1885), and the delightful poem "An Idyl on Ice" (1887).

Most carnivals relied on a volunteer board of directors and committee chairmen and, in more

recent times, a paid executive or managing director. H. P. Wickham, who acted as managing director for both the 1916 and 1917 carnivals, was paid a salary of $1,500.00 for two months work, between December 15, 1916, and February 15, 1917. By January fifteenth, however, Louis Hill was disappointed that Wickham was not working hard enough in producing the Carnival. Hill wrote that the sled dog race hadn't been organized properly, the Seven Corners toboggan slide should be reconsidered, and the Smith Park ice palace should never have been started (Letters from Louis W. Hill, Sr., to H. P. Wickham, February 12, 1916 and January 15, 1917, Hill Papers). Hill, of course, took a very active role in these two Carnivals and expected the same dedication from everybody else involved.

An interior view of the offices for the 1916 Carnival, probably in the St. Paul Athletic Club.

Louis W. Hill, the president of the 1916 and 1917 Carnivals, is shown with a member of the Glacier Park Marching Club.

Although Louis Hill had hoped to "Make it the Hottest One" (which was his proposed motto for a third winter carnival in 1918), only a small parade and festival at Fort Snelling actually took place that year, due to American involvement in World War I. The City of St. Paul took charge of the 1922 Carnival, and businessmen in the Midway neighborhood directed the 1928, 1929 and 1930 festivals. As the Midway event grew, its chairman, Joseph L. Shiely, expressed the hope that it would expand even further:

> *"There are approximately 150,000 people behind this carnival idea… It may take several seasons of effort to build a civic affair here corresponding with the Mardi Gras of New Orleans and the Ak-Sar-Ben in Omaha, but this is only our second year.*

> *"Our committee," he announced, "feels that some civic pageant of magnitude can be built in St. Paul out of our history, rich in Indian lore, combined with our 10,000 lakes, the natural outdoor playground that is Minnesota."* (St. Paul Dispatch, *January 30, 1929*).

Shiely, who recalled participating in the 1896 Carnival as a child, also marched as Boreas Rex VI in 1940.

The final Midway Carnival was held in 1930, but after that, smaller events staged in St. Paul neighborhoods replaced a citywide carnival until 1937. For example, what was billed as the first annual Winter Sports Week was organized by the St. Paul Junior Association of Commerce and held between February 6 and 11, 1935. Sports and snow sculpture were the highlights of the event. A button featuring a ski jumper helped to finance the activities (*St. Paul Daily News,* January 23, 1935, 14).

A new sponsoring organization was formed

when the Winter Carnival was revived in 1937. Another group of St. Paul businessmen felt that the city could benefit from the carnival spirit. And St. Paul felt insulted once again. Another eastern journalist had visited and written something of a disparaging nature in a major national magazine.

The article in *Fortune* was titled "Revolt in the Northwest" and subtitled "The Twin Cities: an examination of Minneapolis and an autopsy of St. Paul." Facts in the article, opinions, and even Ludwig Bemelmans' watercolor views brought controversy, some of which the magazine was able to refute in a later issue. For critics of the Bemelmans slum-angle view of the state capitol, the magazine printed photographs showing that derelict buildings could in fact be seen quite near to the Cass Gilbert masterpiece. But perhaps the most devastating remark was this:

> *People who have moved away sometimes look back upon St. Paul with nostalgia, but if there was a great upheaval of the hills upon which St. Paul is built and the entire city slid into the Mississippi, it would hardly make a ripple in the economic life of the United States of America* (Fortune, *April 1936: 190*).

This time someone wasn't critiquing the weather, but was arguing that St. Paul was corrupt, couldn't attract new business, and was moribund. "In three generations St. Paul has grown up, prospered, and died," wrote *Fortune's* reporter. The new Carnival would have to prove not just that winter could be fun, but that there was somebody alive in St. Paul to enjoy it.

From 1937 through 1942 there were Carnivals like those of the 1880s. The second World War then ended Carnival activities for the duration. In 1946 Saintpaulites, Incorporated, was established, to "advance the educational and civic interests of Saint Paul and its environs; to foster and promote civic interest in sports… to promote and conduct carnivals, expositions, shows, parades, regattas, tournaments…" all for the city's growth and development (Article I of the By-laws of Saintpaulites, Incorporated, in SPWCA Papers, MHS). The Saintpaulites staged the Home Shows, appearances by Bob Hope and Xavier Cugat, and operated the Winter Carnival from 1946 until 1959.

Like its predecessor organizations, the activities of Saintpaulites were supported through memberships, both individual and corporate, sponsorships and, in the case of the carnival, button sales. Names of many officers and directors of Saintpaulites, Incorporated (John F. Scott, William Hickey, Ernest Reiff, J. Perry Dotson) appear later in the lists of Carnival royalty, either as Boreas or Vulcanus.

Walter Van Camp, one of the Executive Directors during the Saintpaulites period, was recruited by the Seattle Seafair festival. Seattle's summertime carnival would also have a story and legend characters named Neptune Rex and the Queen of the Seas.

From 1960 until the financial debacle of the Super Ice Palace, the festival organization was identified by its best known title: the St. Paul Winter Carnival Association. It was a period of both growth and change. Sports competitions often involved national championships. These were also the television years when entertainment stars and entire programs were televised in St. Paul during carnival time. National publicity followed these visiting musicians, actors and actresses, but emphasis on local participation in the festivals decreased as a result.

In 1960 the volunteer support of the Carnival was organized into a Women's Division.

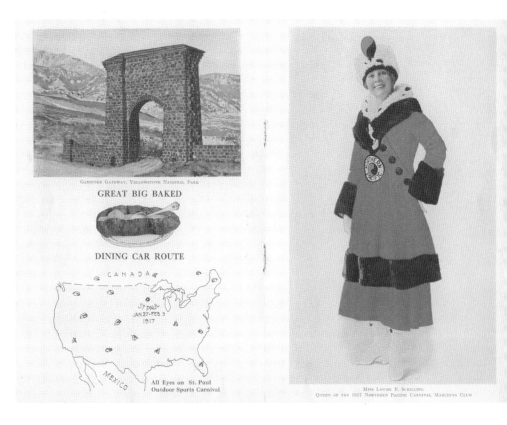

GARDINER GATEWAY, YELLOWSTONE NATIONAL PARK

GREAT BIG BAKED

DINING CAR ROUTE

CANADA

ST PAUL
JAN 27–FEB 3
1917

MEXICO

All Eyes on St. Paul
Outdoor Sports Carnival

MISS LOUISE P. SCHILLING
QUEEN OF THE 1917 NORTHERN PACIFIC CARNIVAL MARCHING CLUB

KSTP

The "Great Big Baked Potato Dining Car Menu" of the Northern Pacific Railroad advertised the 1917 Carnival. Courtesy of Lynn and Walt Hedblum.

Joe Shiely, chairman of the Midway Carnival committee, takes advantage of KSTP radio to publicize the 1929 Carnival. Courtesy of the Midway Chamber of Commerce.

Community Celebration

⚜ **WEAR A** MIDWAY WINTER CARNIVAL · FEB. 2 · FEB. 9 · WHAT'S YOUR NUMBER? · WHO IN 1929? **BUTTON** ⚜

If you want to see

GROVELAND PARK

represented in the Midway Winter Carnival
with a Fireworks celebration at our
Playground Rink next week,

ATTEND THE

Community Meeting
Groveland Park School

MONDAY, JAN. 28, 8 P. M.

Auspices Groveland Park Improvement Association
and the Midway Club

GOOD SPEAKERS!

Show Your Neighborly Spirit!

This 1929 poster indicates the neighborhood nature of the Midway Winter Carnivals. Courtesy of the Midway Chamber of Commerce.

Wives of legend characters as well as those who had played those roles were its members. Membership was expanded in the 1990s to include people without prior Carnival connections, and the group was renamed the "Ambassadors." The Ambassadors have organized a pre-Carnival luncheon for the Queen of the Snows candidates and a luncheon with fashion show in honor of the current queen. Other major activities include assembly of wardrobes for the queen and princesses, and production of the Carnival membership directory. For many years a member of the Ambassadors served as the Queen Mother or chaperone for the Royal Family, especially when they made out-of-town visits.

By the 1970s women were serving on the Board of Directors. Later they were named as festival president (Gloria Schultz in 1989) and as chairman of the board (Judy Cognetta in 1993). Individuals representing the Hispanic, Hmong, and African-American communities were encouraged to participate.

Financial support of the Carnival changed in one significant way during the 1980s. The business community had always supported the Winter Carnival through memberships, sponsorship of events, queen candidates and floats, and the participation of executives in the roles of legend characters. All of this continued, but the businesses tended to be smaller and locally-owned. Queen candidates now had to seek their own sponsors. Sponsorship of events now meant naming rights. As one writer explained, the placement of the name is usually key to the degree of that support. A title sponsor's name comes before the event (the most expensive position), while an event that is "presented by" with the sponsor's name following that of the event means a lesser contribution (*New York Times*, July 16,

1999, C17). And as the writer observed, more and more events, if not entire festivals, now bear a sponsor's name. For example, Pepsi-Cola's contribution in 1992 meant that the proper title of what many called the "Super Ice Palace" was, more accurately, the "Pepsi Ice Palace."

St. Paul businesses, large and small, have supported the Winter Carnival in various ways. They have joined the organization; sponsored a float, marching club or legend character; or provided funds for a specific event. Since those who have assumed the roles of Wind Princes or Princesses, Prime Ministers, Vulcanus, Boreas, or the Queen of the Snows tend to stay involved in Carnival activities, that can become an ongoing connection for a business. There are thus many businesses and their employees with years of involvement in Carnival history. Few, however, can make the claim that they have done so since the beginning. St. Paul's breweries, Hamm's, Schmidt's, and Yoerg's, were all involved until they ceased to operate independently. Minnesota Mining and Manufacturing (3M), so important in today's Carnivals, was not in business in the nineteenth century. Brown & Bigelow was, but took no role in Carnival affairs until 1916. Perhaps the only business with a clear claim to permanent Carnival support is the *St. Paul Pioneer Press*. George Thompson was the publisher of the *St. Paul Dispatch* in 1885 and it was his idea to borrow the Carnival concept from Montreal. *The Dispatch*, once a rival, later became a part of the *Pioneer Press*, and thus can

SPONSORING ORGANIZATIONS	
1885–1899	Ice Palace and Winter Carnival Association
1916–1917	St. Paul Outdoor Sports Carnival Association
1922	St. Paul Municipal Outdoor Sports Association
1928–1930	Midway Club of St. Paul
1935	St. Paul Junior Association of Commerce
1937–1943	St. Paul Winter Carnival Association, Inc.
1946–1959	Saintpaulites, Incorporated
1960–1992	St. Paul Winter Carnival Association
1993–2003	St. Paul Festival and Heritage Foundation

lay claim to support from the opening meeting to this very date.

Those who organize civic festivals belong to the International Festivals and Events Association (IFEA), a group founded in 1956 by the Winter Carnival's John Geisler, Kenneth Walstad of the Minneapolis Aquatennial, Max Colwell of the Tournament of Roses, and Josephine Hauck of the Indy 500 festival. For many years the head-quarters of the IFEA was in Minnesota, staffed by John Geisler and then later by Kenneth Walstad and Nancy Viking.

Another indication of the sophistication of festival management is the fact that a Certified Festival Executive certificate can be earned for a study of civic festivals at Purdue University. During the 1990s this program was exported to other major universities. Today it is possible to earn such a certificate through the Extension School of the University of Minnesota.

As those who direct, support and participate in the St. Paul Winter Carnival consider its heritage and legacy, they can reflect on many elements. The winter sports (skiing, skating and ski jumping) that were virtually unknown a century ago are now familiar to all. Curling was popular in 1886, but tobogganing and snowshoe-ing were a revelation. The Ice Palace built in Central Park was a first for the country. What began in St. Paul was supported by people statewide and later imitated in towns such as New Ulm, Hibbing, and Spicer. Other towns and larger cities would organize their own winter festivals, proving that, after all, an American Siberia might not be such a bad place to live in.

WINTER CARNIVAL PRESIDENTS and CHAIRPERSONS

1886	GEORGE R. FINCH
1887	L. H. MAXFIELD
1888	GEORGE THOMPSON
1889	WILLIAM VAN SLYKE
1896	DR. C. E. BEAN
1899	CHARLES E. FLANDRAU
1916	LOUIS W. HILL, SR.
1917	LOUIS W. HILL, SR.
1922	ERNEST W. JOHNSON
1928	J. L. SHIELY, Chairman
1929	J. L. SHIELY, Chairman
1930	KENNETH M. WRIGHT, Chairman
1935	EUGENE SCOTT and WALTER SEHM, Chairmen
1937	FRANK H. DELANEY
1938	W. C. KENNEY
1939	W. C. KENNEY
1940	LESLIE B. FARRINGTON
1940	WILLIAM J. HICKEY, SR.
1941	WILLIAM J. HICKEY, SR.
1942	WILLIAM J. HICKEY, SR.
1943	ARTHUR DEVINE
1944	C. A. MALEY
1945	C. A. MALEY
1946	C. A. MALEY
1947	WILLIAM J. HICKEY, SR.
1948	JOHN F. SCOTT, SR.
1949	ARTHUR E. EGGERT
1950	CHARLES W. MOORE
1951	LAMBERT S. GILL
1952	ROBERT J. FITZSIMMONS
1953	ROBERT J. FITZSIMMONS
1954	JOSEPH A. ROGERS
1955	HAROLD C. RICHTER
1956	A. LEE RUNYON
1957	L. W. THULIN
1958	JOSEPH A. MAUN
1959	WESLEY M. CHANDLER
1960	WILLIAM C. WOLF
1961	WALTER V. DORLE

1962	JOHN H. DONOHUE, III
1963	WALTER N. NORRIS
1964	PAUL D. EIBERT
1965	WILLIAM A. CURTIS
1966	ROBERT O. ASHBACH
1967	JOHN A. WORKS
1968	B. B. COUNTRYMAN
1969	HARRY W. SETTERGREN
1970	IRWIN R. HANSEN
1971	M. J. GALVIN, JR.
1972	ARMIN BUETOW
1973	ROBERT J. HUBBELL
1974	JACK J. ERDMAN
1975	JAMES R. BELL
1976	EV CARTER
1977	EMMET JOHNSON
1978	M. S. (MIKE) BEDNARZ
1979	BERT J. MCKASY
1980	JAY A. PFAENDER
1981	JOHN A. FISHER
1982	LOU COLLETTE
1983	AL CLASEMAN
1984	RICHARD BARBARI
1985	PATRICK O'NEILL, Chairman of the Board
1985	DARRYL HORSMAN, Festival President
1986	BERT J. MCKASY, Chairman of the Board
1986	BOB CARTER, JR., Festival President
1987	THOMAS CONLIN, Chairman of the Board
1987	JOHN KEMP, Festival President
1988	JOSEPH FRANZGROTE, Chairman of the Board
1988	JOHN ZOBEL, Festival President
1989	DAN OLSON, Chairman of the Board
1989	GLORIA SCHULTZ, Festival President
1990	VICTOR REIM, Chairman of the Board
1990	KENT SHAMBLIN, Festival President
1991	CARL A. KUHRMEYER, Chairman of the Board
1991	JUDY COGNETTA, Festival President
1992	RICHARD ZEHRING, Chairman of the Board
1992	MARK SWANSON, Festival President
1993	JUDY COGNETTA, Chairman of the Board
1993	TED ZWIEG, Festival President
1994	KENT SHAMBLIN, Chairman of the Board
1994	DARRYL ROONEY, Festival Chairman
1995	NEILL O'NEILL, Chairman of the Board
1995	ANNE FORD NELSON, Festival Chairman
1996	ANNE FORD NELSON, Chairman of the Board
1996	JOSEPH JOHNSTON, Festival Chairman
1997	JOSEPH JOHNSTON, Chairman of the Board
1997	GREG NAGAN, Festival Chairman
1998	TED ZWIEG, Chairman of the Board
1998	GREG KUNTZ, Festival Chairman
1999	MARK SWANSON, Chairman of the Board
1999	DAVID CRARY, Festival Chairman
2000	DAN OLSON, Chairman of the Board
2000	JEFF & AMY BOCHE, Festival Chairmen
2001	SAM VERDEJA, Chairman of the Board
2001	CINDY CARVELLI YU, Festival Chairman
2002	STEPHEN SCHMIDT, Chairman of the Board
2002	MONICA GLASS, Festival Chairman
2003	GREG KUNTZ, Chairman of the Board
2003	STACY B. WEISS, Festival Chairman

EXECUTIVE OR MANAGING DIRECTORS

1916–1917	H. P. WICKHAM
1937–1940	MARTIN KELLY
1940–1947	HENRY LUND
1947–1951	WALTER VAN KAMP
1951–1952	FRANK MADDEN
1952–1970	JOHN GEISLER
1970–1983	EUGENE STROMMEN
1983–1986	BOB BONE
1986–1987	TODD MARISKA
1987–1989	TOM CLANCY
1989–1992	BOB CARTER, JR.
1993–1995	ED ALTERMATT
1995–1997	JULIE LYNN SAYOVITZ
1997	— LOU COLLETTE (A board member who served as Executive Director)
1997–1998	STEVE REMINGTON
1998–1999	LOU COLLETTE
1999–2003	ROBERT VIKING

Saint Paul's Frozen Icons

2

The history of Ice Palace architecture, as first explored by Fred Anderes and Ann Agranoff in their book *Ice Palaces* (1983), can be traced to Russia and a cruel czarina. Angry at one of her courtiers Empress Anna Ivanovna sentenced him to be married. She then directed the couple to spend their wedding night in an ice palace she had built on the Neva River during the winter of 1739-1740. The unfortunate couple survived the frigid incarceration and their temporary jail became the rather strange progenitor of ice palaces in North America.

In 1885 when a smallpox epidemic broke out in Montreal, the Winter Carnival planned for this Canadian metropolis in January of 1886 had to be cancelled. It would have been that city's third winter festival with a grand ice palace as its central focus. Learning of the Canadian predicament St. Paul businessmen moved rapidly to organize a winter festival, with the aim of attracting similar enthusiasm and tourism to Minnesota.

Directors of the St. Paul Ice Palace and Winter Carnival Association suggested contacting the Montreal architects for help in designing an Ice Palace. The Hutchinson brothers, A. J. and J. H., were happy to oblige and journeyed to St. Paul to oversee the project in the fall of 1885.

Their design for the 1886 Winter Carnival and the following two Ice Palaces designed by St. Paul architect Charles E. Joy, were the most massive ever built in St. Paul. More than a century later another palace, in 1992, would take away the record for the "tallest ice palace ever built," but the nineteenth century trio set the stage and image for what an Ice Palace should be.

Some ask, "what is a Winter Carnival without an Ice Palace?" Yet, Borealis and Aurora have not always dwelt in such an abode. There have been Ice Palace-less Carnivals, and Winter Carnivals with two buildings of ice. Some Ice Palaces were truly castles while others were called "fortresses" or "forts" since they were hardly more than walls with corner towers. Plans were drawn for Ice Palaces and rejected; and Ice Palaces were begun and not finished due to unseasonably warm weather. Ice, on occasion, was replaced by snow. Taste, weather, and funding have left their mark on the frost-covered dreams of architects and Winter Carnival committees. Nonetheless, St. Paul can take pride in having introduced an important genre of festival architecture to the United States in 1886 and in giving itself an enduring symbol as an icon of its Carnival.

Where an Ice Palace should be built was obviously the first order of business for the 1886 planners. Although not large, Central Park was then considered to be the city's recreational center, so it was an easy choice for the location of the first Ice Palace and many related Carnival activities. Other parks–Como, Phalen, Rice, Highland and Harriet Island–would later be the homes for thousands of ice blocks piled high to make towers, turrets and entrance gates which glistened in the winter sun and disappeared when stormed by the Fire King and his minions (or "gherbers" as one account called them).

Central Park was located north of the downtown area. Its boundary streets were Cedar on the west, Robert to the east, Bluff on the north, and 13th on the south. The 1886 Ice Palace was set in the center of the park, surrounded by rinks for curling and skating and tobogganing slides for children in the streets alongside. Even space for the tepees of the Sioux Indian village could be found within the walls of the Ice Palace.

The style of an Ice Palace, clearly, often magically, reflects the art of its time. Empress Anna's palace was a Palladian villa, 33 feet high, 80 feet long and 23 feet wide. Trees, carved of ice and painted, surrounded the palace while ice sculptures stood in niches along the façade. The graceful design seemed appropriate for a summer residence, a dacha perhaps set in the woods of a country estate.

The Ice Palace built in Montreal dwarfed the early Russian effort. The Hutchinson brothers first designed a huge civic structure which, if built of brick or granite, could easily serve as a city hall, courthouse, railroad station, or post office. A large tower loomed in the center. Rooms of various dimensions spread around its base. Surrounded by thick walls, the area offered spaces for crowds eager to march or enjoy the winter sports offered. Arched gateways led into the complex.

For those who saw the Ice Palaces of the 1880s in Montreal or St. Paul the sheer size was part of the amazing achievement. But there was more. Electric lights, unusual at the time, created a rainbow effect on the ice blocks. When the ritual storming of the palace took place, rockets and other fireworks lit the sky, causing the ice to shine in spectacular colors, bringing magic to a winter night.

For St. Paul's Winter Carnivals of 1886, 1887, and 1888 there were Ice Palaces, the first built from the Montreal plans and the next two from the plans of Charles E. Joy of St. Paul. Joy designed a palace for 1889 which was not built due to warm weather. He was then hired by the winter festival committee in Leadville, Colorado, to design an ice palace for them.

The 1886 Hutchinson palace, the beginning of the tradition, was really the plainest of the group. A tall central tower with long slits breaking its solidity was surrounded by a wall and entered through an arch. Once inside the wall visitors could choose between a curling rink, three toboggan slides, and two skating rinks. Warming rooms were provided which gave space to a lunch counter, vendors of cigars, candy, and nuts, and even display space for the "Greely relics" (*St. Paul Daily Globe*, February 11, 12, 1886). The Carnival committee had invited Arctic explorer Adolphus Washington Greely, but instead, an exhibit of

Evening view of the 1886 ice palace, the first in the United States. From "The Royal Route", a sales brochure of the Chicago, St. Paul & Omaha Railroad.

The 1887 ice palace in a drawing from the "Northwestern Architect Supplement." Courtesy of the St. Paul Public Library.

relics (his sled, almanac, dogskin gloves and seal – skin boots, among other things) from his recent expedition came, along with his regrets. After spending three years marooned in the Arctic, coming to Minnesota for a cold vacation may not have appealed to Lt. Greely. A larger display of Greely materials appeared at the Chicago World's Fair of 1893, seven years later.

The next Ice Palace had an octagonal tower, supported by neat flying buttresses around its base. Its wall had ceremonial entrance gates, one topped by a seated Borealis Rex welcoming all to his realm. This 1887 palace was famed for its interior spaces, hallways, and even a maze, modeled after that of the Hampton Court Palace, near London. The maze would later inspire author F.

Scott Fitzgerald. The last of these three palaces, in 1888, had a round central tower with one side arranged to display examples of the ice carver's art.

Massive central towers or slender turrets emerge from the ice block bases of every later Ice Palace. They mark junctures of walls or the termini of a plan's arms. In the palaces of the late 1930s each tower had its own identity: King's Tower, Queen's Tower, and so on, as they did in the 1986 and 1992 palaces. Architect Bill Rust dedicated four of the towers in his Harriet Island design to the Wind Princes, carrying out the concept in the color of the canvas canopies. Seven lesser towers in the Rust design referred to the topography of St. Paul, which is, like Rome, a "City on Seven Hills." The central tower represented Boreas whose palace it was.

A major problem for every Winter Carnival committee has been the weather. Winter is supposed to be cold in Minnesota, but just when the freezing temperatures are needed, warm, melting days sometimes arrive instead. The first Winter Carnival, scheduled to be a New Year's day event, had to be moved to a late January commencement date when the cold weather did not arrive. But then winter changed its mind and gave Borealis both a blizzard and sub zero temperatures for his first year. A writer for *Harper's Weekly* wrote about that predicament and then joked that other problems concerned St. Paul's planners. He said they worried that ice left outdoors could crumble, ice bugs were nibbling on the foundations of the palace, dry rot had set in, and even worse, stacked ice had caught fire, destroying the palace (*Harper's Weekly*, February 20, 1886, 119). But the Ice Palace, "unreal and fairy-like," was built and served as a landmark, a sign-post indicating "Here's where the fun takes place."

A planned carnival with an Ice Palace had to be cancelled in 1889, and postponed and then cancelled once more in 1890 when temperatures rose. In 1889 not only had a Carnival Committee been organized, but a handsome pre-Carnival program was already in print, and plans for the Ice Palace publicized. Carnival president William A. Van Slyke cancelled the festival with profound regret.

As the Table at the end of this chapter indicates, St. Paul's next palace (in 1896) was a much simpler affair. It was a backdrop for ceremonies rather than a true residence. While it could be argued that the original plan did not call for a palace on the scale of the 1880s edifices, the

The inside entrance of the 1896 Fort Karnival ice palace, on Aurora Avenue between St. Albion and Avon streets. Courtesy of John Meyers.

height of the 1896 ice structure was curtailed by the weather. However, enough was achieved to give the idea. One description of the 1896 Ice Palace read:

Fort Karnival is an ice palace for those who want plenty of ice for their winter pleasures, and merely an enclosure for the purpose of carrying on Carnival sports for those who do not want an ice palace… Fort Karnival was barely ready at 9 o'clock last evening, but it was ready and that was all that could be asked.

By the time the day crew on construction got to work yesterday morning there was apparently a week's work before them. The big gaps in the walls had been closed with blocks of ice, the chevaux de frise [defensive obstacle] that had finished off the top of the wall had been placed and each point was ornamented with an American flag. The finishing touches had been given to the medieval towers about the portal and thereon had been displayed until one's eyes ached in trying to count them. It is uphill work to build an ice palace when the ice keeps melting in the hands of the workmen, but it can be done. And it was done (The Daily Pioneer Press, January 21, 1896, 2).

The whole interior was a blaze of light, making it easy to watch the two rinks full of skaters and the avid tobogganers climbing up sixty feet to the top of the toboggan before sliding down 600 feet to the end of the run.

The 1899 Winter Carnival was opposed by the city's Chamber of Commerce and business owners located near Smith (now, Mears) Park, where it was suggested that the Ice Palace might be located. The Carnival committee hoped to have the lighting and fireworks be more prominent and that worried local merchants. Allen

The 1917 Ice Palace in Rice Park. The St. Paul public library is at the left. Courtesy of The J. J. Hill Library.

The 1917 Town and Country Club Ice Palace. Courtesy of the Minnesota Historical Society.

Stem designed a palace for the 1899 Carnival, but only a button (which all collectors covet) was prepared that year since the weather was too warm for building a palace. Most members of the committee agreed that a Carnival without an Ice Palace "would be much like Hamlet without the prince of Denmark" (*St. Paul Dispatch*, January 10, 1900). In the end the Carnival was cancelled.

Although the legend called for the Fire King to storm the Ice King's "abode," that residence became even more modest in 1916 and 1917. The emphasis in the two Louis W. Hill – organized Carnivals was on the sporting events and the parades rather than on the Ice Palace. In 1916 Fort Karnival was built on Harriet Island. Since the largest group of parade participants represented

Hill's Northern Pacific railroad under the banner of "Glacier Park," a western fort structure seemed appropriate. While earlier palaces had icy rooms, the fort on Harriet Island had tepees to serve as warming houses. Fires could be lit inside and benches were placed where skaters could pause to change from shoes to skates. The following year the tepee poles were salvaged to hold flags on the Rice Park ice palace walls.

There were two official palaces in 1917. For the queens there was a heart-shaped wall in Rice Park and the second, more traditional, palace was set on a hill west of today's third tee of the golf course, at the Town and Country Club. Rice Park's effort was a simple wall merely enclosing a space for skating. An Ice Palace was also contem-

Model for the 1930 Ice Palace. Courtesy of the Midway Chamber of Commerce.

The 1930 royalty pose at the front of the Midway Ice Palace. Courtesy of the Midway Chamber of Commerce.

plated for Smith (now, Mears) Park, but was not built as an economy measure. The Town and Country Club's palace served as the ceremonial site. Parades marched past it, the Fire King's troops stormed it, and documentary movie filmmakers focused their lenses on it.

Given the Town and Country Club's long involvement with the Winter Carnival staging the parades and pageant there seemed right. That involvement began with the Nushka Club, one of the winter marching clubs formed to participate in the first Winter Carnivals. They marched in their red and black blanket suits with polar bear insignia on the jackets, skated, tramped, tobogganed, and finally felt the fun and outdoor sports should continue throughout the year. By 1890 the Nushkas, now organized as the Town and Country Club, had a headquarters building designed by Cass Gilbert. Through the years members of the Club directed the business of later carnivals and wore the royal robes of Boreas Rex.

Only one of the three Midway carnivals (1928 – 1930) had an Ice Palace. One of St. Paul's major architectural firms, now known as Ellerbe Becket, Inc., designed a tall, turreted wall with side wings for King Boreas and his Queen Midway in 1930. It was built at Dunning field, near Selby and Snelling avenues, and faced a skating rink where some of the Carnival Indian pageantry took place.

St. Paul's parks, clubs, and playgrounds weren't the only places to house Ice Palaces. As early as 1887 the city of West St. Paul had its own Fort Karnival. A twenty-five-foot-high blockhouse served as a storage site for the necessary fireworks. There was a stockade for Sioux Indians inside the walls and first class toboggan slides. While ladies and gentlemen had separate "retiring rooms," both could enjoy the oyster bar and band concerts. As

the accompanying table shows, White Bear Lake, Red Wing, Hibbing, and New Ulm have all hosted Ice Palace architecture. Spicer, whose Green Lake has been the place to harvest especially clear ice, has naturally been home to Ice Palaces. These palaces have usually been, like St. Paul's, the focal point of a local winter festival.

Where to harvest the ice for a palace has been a concern for every carnival contractor. Artificial

The 1887 West St. Paul Ice Palace, from the Winter Carnival Edition of the Northwest Magazine. *Courtesy of the Minnesota Historical Society.*

H. G. BRANT
ASSISTANT POSTMASTER
SAINT PAUL, MINN.

MAILED FROM THE ICE PALACE

SAINT PAUL WINTER CARNIVAL

SAINT PAUL
FEB 3
12³⁰ PM
1940
MINN.

Mr. Arthur O'Brien.
Adjt. General's Office.
State Capitol.
St. Paul, Minnesota.

UNITED STATES POST OFFICE
ICE PALACE BRANCH
COME IN—WRITE A LETTER
SPECIAL CACHET
FOR ALL LETTERS MAILED HERE
3¢ LOCAL DELIVERY 2¢

Specially prepared envelope mailed at the 1940 Ice Palace. Courtesy of Tom Reiersgord.

The 1940 Ice Palace, in which a branch of the United States post office was located. Courtesy of Ramsey County Historical Society.

"solely of coagulated Mississippi water!" (*St. Paul Daily Globe*, February 8, 1886, 1). Later, Como and Phalen lakes were to supply the palace builders with ice, but Spicer's Green Lake was often said to provide the best quality ice. River ice, if necessary, would be a second class choice as it tended to be somewhat dirtier and darker in hue. In 1992 visitors to the Harriet Island site could look past the carefully protected Green Lake blocks to note the unfrozen Mississippi River flowing past.

In the early days ice harvested from a distant lake was covered in straw or sawdust and delivered to the building site by horse and wagon. The delivery system is now motorized with the ice loaded into semitrailers, but some of the other steps in harvesting and handling blocks of ice have not changed that much. Cutting the ice is still done with ice saws, ice blocks are lifted by large tongs and the blocks may be stored in cold water while awaiting use. While it waits, the ice will gain strength and density. For the 1992 Harriet Island Ice Palace blocks of ice were lifted by forklifts into washing tanks. Ice blocks harvested from lakes have an irregular surface due to the action of wind and snow. Thus, ice blocks must be scraped and cleaned in the tanks so that the top of each block will be smooth. Finally, the blocks are delivered to the proper location either on water in wooden chutes or by conveyor belts inside the chutes.

Building an Ice Palace calls upon the skills of architects, engineers, ice cutters, lighting designers, and masons, among other trades. On occasion (as in 1986) many workers have volunteered their time, but for the 1930s Ice Palaces funding was available through the Works Progress Administration (WPA). Unemployed construction workers were hired through the city of St.

ice has long been a possibility but local lakes were usually the source for the nineteenth century palace builders. For the 1886 palace special ice blocks "of crystal clearness" were presented by citizens of White Bear Lake, Stillwater, St. Peter, Bismarck, Fargo, and Ortonville. Most of the palace was built, as humorist Bill Nye wrote,

Paul's public works department and assigned to build the Ice Palace and the Carnival toboggan slides, thus providing jobs and assisting the WPA's winter recreation program (*St. Paul Dispatch*, January 6, 1936).

For the period from 1937 to 1947, while Charles Bassford served as city architect, the draftsman who did most of the creative work on the ice palaces was Clarence (Cap) W. Wigington, one of the city's first black architects. Wigington designed park and playground structures, schools, the Holman field administration building, the Highland Park water tower, and the pavilion on Harriet Island now named for him. According to his daughters, Wigington's favorite projects were the palaces he designed for each of the six Winter Carnivals held in that ten year stretch. They told Bob Olsen that their father whistled cheerfully like the sound of a teakettle while he worked on the palace drawings. (Colored renderings for these palaces are now in the Clarence Wigington Papers at the University of Minnesota's Northwest Architectural Archives.) But not all of his designs were realized. Other architects were responsible for the 1938 and 1939 castles and in 1942 and 1947 warm weather meant that Boreas' temporary homes could not be completed. There were no carnivals held during the World War II years of 1944 and 1945.

The thick walls and huge central towers vanished from Ice Palace design by the late 1930s. A new architectural style called for different solutions and that style was Art Deco, or its subcategory, "Art Moderne." It was a much more geometric approach, with the Ice Palaces becoming symmetrical, with undulating walls, linear curtains, and even growing small eastern domes as in the 1939 Como Park palace. There were numerous towers, ending in parapets, although none stood as tall as in the 1880s. The central tower's façade was emphasized by a portico suggesting the entrance to a school, something Wigington had often designed. Visitors could walk around these palaces, but, except for the post office branch in the 1940 palace, there were no longer rooms of any kind for the public to enter. The palaces were simply backdrops for Carnival events. At Mounds Park, in 1938, the concept of a "palace" was replaced by two semicircular ice disks, one sixty feet tall and, in front of that, another disk fifty feet high. Although Cap Wigington had drawn two traditional palaces for that year the committee wanted a far simpler stage-set since they had invited Swedish skating star Vivi-anne Hulten to perform and this would

The 1939 Ice Palace at Como Park.

after that, planners arranged for the Ice Palaces to stand tall and regally north of downtown (Como Park), west (Highland Park), and in downtown itself, in Rice Park, in Town Square, and on the Kellogg Mall, just above the Mississippi River. Locations for ice palaces, Carnival activities, parking and transportation would become harder to find as buildings and sculpture were located in the parks.

Como Park (in 1939, 1940, and 1941) proved to be a good choice. These Ice Palaces were built on the west shore of the lake near to the pavilion. The first was an Arabian Night fantasy designed by Milton Bergstedt. The other two were Cap Wigington designs, which took advantage of a hill above the pavilion for emphasis. Wigington's designs for 1940 and 1941 connected large towers with double walls. Lighting technicians could arrange their strands of bulbs so that the colored lights glowed through the ice and window spaces. These palaces sheltered courtyards with ice thrones for ceremonial use.

For both the last prewar and the first major postwar Carnivals Cap Wigington designed Ice Palaces to be built in Highland Park. In both years the weather did not cooperate and the two palaces had to be demolished before Vulcan and his Krewe could truly attack. So that the 1942 Queen of the Snows would not feel cheated, her hometown offered what St. Paul could not provide. After a parade through Centerville, in Anoka County, Queen Martha Dupuis and her King, Lambert Gill (Boreas Rex VIII) were escorted to ice thrones before an ice wall at Centerville High School (*St. Paul Pioneer Press*, February 4, 1942).

For almost thirty years following the second World War Ice Palaces were a lost art. Boreas' castle had to be symbolized by small towers or

Architect's drawing of the 1941 Ice Palace. Courtesy of the Ramsey County Historical Society.

View of the 1941 Como Park Ice Palace, as actually constructed.

be her venue. Flanking the large sheet of ice were ice colonnades with pennants flying from poles. This added color and contrast to the glistening white scene as canopies do on palace towers.

With the revival of the Winter Carnival in 1937 events as well as ice structures were commonly located throughout St. Paul's neighborhoods. The 1937 Ice Palace stood across the street from the State Capitol, repeating the earliest palace sites in the eight acres of Central Park. But diminutive walls, and the material was often snow rather than ice. A high school teacher from Michigan was the architect and contractor for a series of snow palaces erected between 1967 and 1971 on Kellogg Boulevard between Cedar and Minnesota streets. Parker Seiler had been doing snow sculpture when he decided to visit St. Paul in search of new opportunities. He met John Geisler, then managing director of the Carnival, and was offered room, board, and $15.00 per day to make snow sculptures in Como Park.

Seiler's first effort was a snow statue of a clown in a car. Seiler recalled that at first there was so little snow that ice chips had to be harvested from a nearby skating rink, but then four inches of snow fell so his clown could be fully devel-

oped. A photograph of his work was used on the cover of the city's telephone book in 1964. From sculpture Seiler moved on to do a series of small snow castles, each with a maximum height of 36 feet. Snow and water were usually frozen in blocks, then trucked to the site of his Kellogg Boulevard palaces. Two or three people usually assisted Seiler. One year an assistant was Bob Olsen, then a student at St. Olaf College in Northfield. Olsen later felt that the Winter Carnival needed to rediscover its heritage. It was time for another Ice Palace, and John Geisler agreed with Olsen's proposal.

Olsen's palace, of manufactured ice, was built on Harriet Island not far from Cap Wigington's pavilion. It was intended to suggest the castles of

Evening view of the 1948 Como Park Ice Palace. Courtesy of Steve Shumaker.

the 1880s even though its tallest tower was only thirty-six feet high. It was certainly the only Ice Palace ever built which obtained college credit for its builder. Working on the Ice Palace started Olsen on a lifelong path of Carnival research.

In 1976 the Winter Carnival and the St. Paul chapter of the American Institute of Architects held an Ice Palace competition for a Bicentennial edifice. Jerry Zuber and Craig Rafferty's plans won and their palace was erected downtown, in what would later be renamed as Town Square. The 1976 Ice Palace was a structure of walls, not towers, described as a modern interpretation of the palaces of the past.

The Centennial palace of 1986 was something quite different. It was a record-setter, both for its height and for its volunteer support. In

1947 Carnival officers complained that the $11,000 which they had just spent to build an ice palace (which melted!) was more than they had planned. Finances became much more of a problem with both the 1986 Centennial and 1992 Super Bowl palaces.

For the Winter Carnival's centennial in 1986 an Ice Palace was expected and required. A century deserved that sort of marker. The location, however, would be different. The chairman of the Ice Palace committee was Charlie Hall, who had served as Boreas Rex XLVII three years earlier. He recalled a knighting ceremony he had conducted at Lake Phalen while he was the Ice King and thought that park should be considered as the site. The eventual spot selected was on a four acre island along that lake's west shore.

Construction of the 1969 Snow Palace.

The 1967 Snow Palace.

Architect's drawing for the 1976 Ice Palace.

A statewide competition was held and an architect from the Ellerbe firm, Karl Ermanis, was selected as the winner. This would be Ellerbe's third Ice Palace, following the simple wall of 1930 and the Arabian Nights castle of 1939. Ermanis' design, as befits a centennial, was totally different from anything built before. His towers were sharp, pointed shafts, more like obelisks than the fat bastions of the 1880s. The curved surfaces made it difficult to build and eventually some of them were eliminated so that the palace could be finished before the official closing of the Carnival.

The designs were judged on creativity, potential for construction, and interpretation of the Winter Carnival legend. In the Ellerbe design towers for each of the four winds matched their "power and temperament." The tallest tower, which would have reached 150 feet, could not be completed. A spell of warm weather caused its de-mise. Nonetheless, the central remaining tower did measure 128' 9" and that was enough for inclusion in the Guinness Book of Records as the tallest manmade structure built of ice. The palace won awards for its design from the Minnesota chapter of the American Institute of Architects, for its engineering excellence from the Consulting Engineers Council of Minnesota, and as a work of public art from the Twin Cities Mayors. Although it was ephemeral, it was a work of enchantment that over one million people went to see.

One advantage of the island location was that the ice could be harvested from Lake Phalen and be returned to its waters after the storming by the Vulcans. It also meant that visitors could stand in the park to view the ice palace, viewing its spires through a filter of trees.

The financing of the Ice Palace was arranged in a variety of ways: funds from the Winter Carnival, sales of $10.00 blocks of ice for which a handsome certificate was the permanent record and receipt, and volunteer labor from the St. Paul Building and Trades unions. The architects insisted on errors and omissions insurance coverage which was one of the hardest financial problems to solve. Eventually one insurance company agreed to provide the policy and WTCN (Channel 11) donated the $50,000.00 for the premium.

Building the 1986 Ice Palace proved to be a learning experience. First, a concrete slab on pilings was needed to support the palace on the soft soil of the island, a concept also followed for the 1992 palace. Old ice cutting tools (found in Colorado) and the advice of an experienced ice cutter named Ed Chaput solved the harvesting of ice from the lake. Cold weather and then warm days meant that some aspects of the original plan could not be built so the architect redrew them. Unlike the Highland Park palaces in 1942 and 1947, however, the Phalen Park Centennial Palace was completed. For the public the results vastly justified the project. The

Ice Block Certificate used to finance the 1986 Ice Palace. Design shows the first Ice Palace, of 1886. Courtesy of Bob Fletcher, Sr.

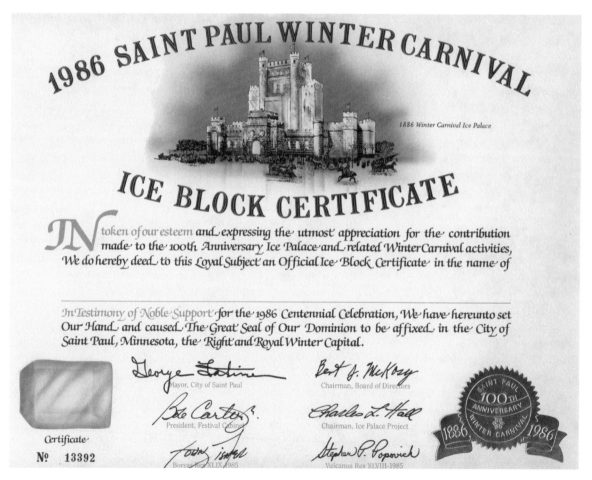

Palace was a glistening, wondrous sight bathed in multi-colored lights throughout its three week lifespan. The height provided one problem for the Vulcans whose duty it was to storm and destroy the Palace. Too tall for mere men to attack, instead they aimed red dyed water at the main tower to symbolize their attack before the wrecking ball did its work.

One couple who saw the Ice Palace just before it was demolished decided to preserve the memory. George and Jeanette Gru built their replica of stained glass, using a copy of the original Ellerbe drawings. The Grus' palace, scaled at 3/8" to 1 inch, is lighted as was the original, and is now on display at the Minnesota Historical Society in its "Weather Permitting" exhibit.

In 1988 Bill Rust of White Bear Lake designed a smaller palace on Harriet Island which stood near the unique volcano for Vulcanus. This was a snow mountain, sixty feet tall, with an ice wall on its summit. A scissors lift raised a sixteen-foot tall figure of Vulcanus to the top of the snow volcano so he could wave his three-foot long sword and hurl threats at an ice figure of Boreas nearby. After the Carnival the Vulcanus figure had several more years of active life as Frankenstein at a park near Forest Lake.

A long lobbying campaign brought the Super Bowl to the Minneapolis Metrodome in 1992. One of the arguments which convinced the National Football League to schedule the championship game in chilly Minnesota was the fact that Super Sunday would coincide with the Winter Carnival. Certainly out-of-town guests would come to St. Paul if they could see an ice palace and so the Super Ice Palace project headed by John Zobel, a former Vulcanus Rex, was launched.

Architect Bill Rust and contractor Tom Keller had worked together on the earlier Harriet Island

castle and volcano; Keller had worked on the Phalen Park palace as well. Their expertise would be needed on the Super Ice Palace. Ice for the palace came from Spicer's Green Lake. Local trade unions provided the workers and Pepsi-Cola was the major source of funds. The design placed twelve towers along two walls which intersected. The tallest tower, which reached 166' 8", was placed at the intersection. Ice columns led the way to the false grand entrance for, like other twentieth century palaces, the Super Ice Palace could not be entered. Space existed within its walls, but only for lighting, which was computer-programmed like that on the 1986 palace.

The light show turned the towers from red to green, to yellow, and then blue. Above each tower was a jaunty canopy with a pennant flying at the top. Over 200 shallow niches were carved into the palace's towers, to suggest windows. People living on the west side had an especially good view of the palace from the bluffs.

Those who wanted to visit the palace were encouraged to park and ride a shuttle bus, without charge for wearers of Carnival buttons. The system worked, thousands of visitors did as requested, but there were not enough buttons, and no way to charge those who lacked them. This transportation provided an extra cost, but there were other cost overruns as well.

The total cost of the project was $1,900,000.00, twice as much as had been budgeted and raised.

Tom Keller, Charlie Hall, and Bob Fletcher, Sr., mark the official completion from the top of the 1986 Ice Palace. Courtesy of Bob Fletcher, Sr.

By August, 1992, the Carnival board of directors was still seeking $300,000.00 in donations. The debt was eventually settled, but only after some of the creditors agreed to write-off part of the sums owed, and a law suit brought by the architect, the company that supplied the ice (Wee-Kut of New London, Minnesota) and Metropolitan Steel Fabricators of White Bear Lake (who supplied the steel scaffolding) against the Carnival organizations was settled (*St. Paul Pioneer Press*, August 15, 1992 and November 8, 1994, 1C).

The problems presented by the Super Ice Palace led to a restructuring of the Carnival organization. The executive director resigned in the summer of 1992; his successors all served brief terms until 1999 when Robert Viking became CEO and president of the Saint Paul Festival and Heritage Foundation.

It was a sour aftermath to a beautiful achievement, but the Winter Carnival has continued and may have yet more ice palaces in its future. As architectural historian Larry Millett once wrote, the Ice Palace:

> is much more than an appropriate symbol of this area's climate. It also expresses the community's spirit, an expression that is particularly strong because the palace truly is a people's project, built by hundreds of volunteers and financed by thousands of small donations (St. Paul Pioneer Press and Dispatch, February 7, 1986).

Building an Ice Palace has never been a yearly event nor is it a project undertaken without adequate time and preparation. In 2004 St. Paul planned to host the National Hockey League All-Star game and celebrate the 150th anniversary of the earliest Minnesota tourist promotion, the Grand River Excursion of 1854. It seemed a good moment to undertake another Ice Palace.

Planning began with obtaining pledges for pro bono work from an architectural firm (Setter Leech Lindstrom/ Leo A. Daly), Collins Electrical, a contractor (Kraus-Anderson), the St. Paul building trades unions, and others. Those pledges were huge commitments, but still needed were studies on the feasibility of a downtown location for the Ice Palace. The Minnesota Wild, St. Paul's NHL hockey team and local host of the All-Star game, had its offices in the old Minnesota Club, and played its games in the Xcel Energy Center, so clearly it preferred a downtown palace. Parking and transportation for both the expected 500,000 visitors and those who work downtown needed to be resolved in advance. The Saint Paul Festival and Heritage Association board of directors determined that funding, logistics, and transportation questions should all be fully resolved before it voted to permit the construction. On April 30, 2003, the board voted "Yes."

If built, the design proposed by Frank Anderson of SLL/Leo A. Daly would be located just north of the Xcel Energy Center. A fifteen-foot tall wall would surround the site and the 5 to 6 story high Ice Palace. The palace would not be as tall as those of 1986 or 1992, but it would also be the first in many years which could be entered by visitors (*St. Paul Pioneer Press*, March 9, 2003, 1A). For all those lucky enough to visit it, this Ice Palace, like its predecessors, would be a sight to remember.

SAINT PAUL
WINTER CARNIVAL
✳ *1992 Ice Castle* ✳

Architect's drawing of the 1992 Ice Palace.

ST. PAUL ICE AND SNOW STRUCTURES

YEAR	CONTRACTOR/ DESIGNER/ ARCHITECT	DIMENSIONS: H x W x L (in feet)	COMMENTS: LOCATION	BLOCKS OF ICE	LABOR/TIME	COST
1886	A. C. Hutchison James Brodie, contractor	106 x 154 x 180	Central Park	20,000 blocks	200 men/3 weeks	$5,210
1886	Brinckerhoff and Phillips. F. Althen, contractor	54 high, 24 at base	Kelly Park near Euclid Avenue, Dayton's Bluff, Crystal Ice tower			$700
1887	Charles E. Joy Taylor & Craig, contractors	140 x 194 x 217	Central Park	35,000 blocks	—	$7,500
1888	Teltz & Joy, architects, Taylor & Craig, contractors	130 x 190 x 195	Central Park	55,000 blocks	—	$12,500
1889	Teltz & Joy, architects	—	Planned but not built			
1896	Major Wilkinson Rheaume & St. Pierre, contractors	40 x 660 x 300	Aurora Avenue, between St. Albans & Avon "Fort Karnival"			
1899	A. H. Stem	—	West Bank Mississippi River	Planned but not built		
1900	A. H. Stem	—	West Bank Mississippi River	Planned but not built		
1916	—	12 or 16	Harriet Island		—	
1917	People's Coal & Ice Co. A. R. Jackson, superintendent	14	Rice Park Queen's palace	—		$600
1917	People's Coal & Ice Co. A.R. Jackson, superintendent	—	Town & Country Club	—		$600
1930	Ellerbe & Co. A.M. Sandberg, contractor	40 x 100	Dunning Field, Marshall near Lexington	300 tons of ice		
1937	C. W. Wigington + Charles Bassford	70 x 193 x 86	Capitol Mall	30,000 blocks	Art Deco design	
1938	Jack Horner	60 and 50	Mounds Park	20,000 blocks	Two semi-circular disks	
1938	?		Dayton's Bluff	Tower		
1939	Milton Bergstedt/ Ellerbe Architects	80 x 240	Como Park, south of pavilion on west shore Arabian Nights fortress	18,000 blocks		

YEAR	CONTRACTOR/ DESIGNER/ ARCHITECT	DIMENSIONS: H x W x L (in feet)	COMMENTS: LOCATION	BLOCKS OF ICE	LABOR/TIME	COST
1940	C. W. Wigington	75 x 150 x 42	Como Park on hill west of pavilion, on west shore		50 men	$14,000
1940	C. W. Wigington	?	Courthouse Square	Fire King ice throne		
1941	C. W. Wigington	80 x 123 x 123	Como Park On hill west of pavilion, on west shore	22,000 blocks		
1942	C. W. Wigington	?	Highland Park Golf Course 2/3rds done, melted			
1947	C. W. Wigington + R. G. Zelzer	?	Highland Park Golf Course 1/3 done, destroyed			
1948	—	15 x 200	Como Park Ice wall around Pavilion, with throne			
1949	Clement F. Scully Equipment Company	20 x 40 x 40	Victory Square, 4th & Wabasha street	Ice blocks over frame		
1950	—	?	Victory Square behind throne	4 pillars and ice frame		$11,000
1952	—	?	Rice Park			
1967	Parker Seiler	36	Kellogg Blvd. between Cedar & Minnesota streets	packed snow		
1968	Parker Seiler	36	Kellogg Blvd. between Cedar & Minnesota streets	packed snow		
1969	Parker Seiler	36	Kellogg Blvd. between Cedar & Minnesota streets	packed snow		
1970	Parker Seiler	36	Kellogg Blvd. between Cedar & Minnesota streets	packed snow		
1971	Parker Seiler	36	Kellogg Blvd. between Cedar & Minnesota streets	packed snow		
1972	Parker Seiler	36	Kellogg Blvd. Between Cedar & Minnesota streets	packed snow		
1975	Bob Olsen	36 x 100 x 42	Harriet Island	1,600 blocks medieval castle		$13,900
1976	Craig Rafferty & Jerry Zuber, architects; Sheehy Construction, contractor	40 x 104 x 93	Town Square	1,964 blocks modern interpretation of 1886 castle		$23,000
1986	Karl Ermanis/ Ellerbe Architects; Austin M. Keller, contractor	128' 9" x 90 x 90	Phalen Park	9,000 blocks	750 men	$200,000

ST. PAUL ICE AND SNOW STRUCTURES

YEAR	CONTRACTOR/ DESIGNER/ ARCHITECT	DIMENSIONS: H x W x L (in feet)	COMMENTS: LOCATION	BLOCKS OF ICE	LABOR/TIME	COST
1988	Rust Architects Austin M. Keller, contractor	60 x 200	Harriet Island, Mt. Vulcanus	200 tons of packed snow with 10' ice wall on top		
1988	Rust Architects Austin M. Keller, contractor	40	Harriet Island, "Castle of the Winds"	Seven towers and two ice thrones		
1992	Rust Architects Austin M. Keller, contractor	166' 8" x 249 x 170	Harriet Island	18,000 blocks		$1,100,000

OUTSTATE MINNESOTA ICE AND SNOW STRUCTURES

YEAR	CONTRACTOR/ DESIGNER/ ARCHITECT	DIMENSIONS: H x W x L (in feet)	COMMENTS: LOCATION	BLOCKS OF ICE		
1887	W. H. Castner + W. J. Yanish	40	West St. Paul			
1896	Julius Berndt	42 x 86	New Ulm, North German Park			
1921	?	?	Hibbing, near old Great Northern station			
1928	F. O. Green	20	Red Wing, Broadway Park	1,000 blocks		
1935	—	?	White Bear Lake, Railroad Park Built around the bandstand			
1939	U.S. Forest Service and CCC workers	100 long	Bemidji, Lake Bemidji at foot of Third street			
1942	—	10	Centerville, High school Ice throne			
1987	Gideon Doty + Mike Lint	27	Spicer, Green Lake shoreline "Engwall Castle"	1,500 blocks	15-20 workers	170 tons of ice
1988	Gideon Doty + Carl Engwall	?	Spicer, Green Lake shoreline	1,000 blocks		
1993	Wee Kut Ice Co.	40	Spicer, Green Lake shoreline	1,200 blocks		
1993	Rust Architects	10 x 85 x 56	White Bear Lake, Highway 61 between 2nd and 4th streets	1,001 blocks		
1994	Rust Architects	35 x 82	White Bear Lake, Highway 61 between 2nd and 4th streets			

Carved in Ice, Shaped in Snow

Sculpture using winter's materials of ice or snow has been part of most carnivals since 1886. Over the entrance archway to a palace, in niches on façades, or on pedestals in Central Park, carvers placed intricate examples of their art. Virtually any subject could be carved and, with luck, might survive until the end of the festival. Carvers created the classical (a discus thrower or a Venus de Medici), the seasonal (a snowshoer in club uniform), and the patriotic (a bust of Abraham Lincoln), all long before anyone felt that the repertoire could only include polar bears or snowmen.

Along city streets in 1886 carvers placed a Statue of Liberty, a woman in a toboggan costume, and an Indian on horseback spearing a buffalo, as well as ice arches, one of which had icy heads of buffalo, deer, and sheep, as ornamentation. White Bear Lake citizens sent two winter statues for St. Paul: a cub carved of ice and a full-sized bear created from a block of frozen milk. Both were placed near the palace.

One early ice sculptor was A. F. Lewis, to whom work at both the 1886 and 1887 Carnivals was attributed. He created his marvels with "nothing but a common ax" (*St. Paul and Minneapolis Pioneer Press*, January 18, 1887). Some carvers were invited to do their work while at other times competitions were staged. In 1887 ice placed outside the palace walls and near to the giant bust of Abraham Lincoln was intended for school children to carve.

Downtown parks have often been the sites for ice sculpture. R. J. Harper of the St. Paul Institute carved four polar bears in 1917 to stand guard outside the Queen's palace in Rice Park. In 1937

1887 sculpture of a St. George's Snowshoe Club member on a downtown sidewalk.

an itinerant German artist came to St. Paul and offered to create something for the Carnival. Josef Edlbauer had done snow sculptures the previous year for the Winter Olympics at Garmisch – Partenkirchen, Germany. American friends persuaded him to come to Minnesota to find work. In what was then known as old Courthouse Square, Edlbauer completed a snow sculpture of Ben Hur standing in his chariot, pulled by four horses (*St. Paul Dispatch*, January 14, 1937).

Other invited artists have included Foster Kienholz who created another set of ice sculp-

Both snow and ice sculpture had become better known disciplines by the 1980s. Other winter festivals had displays and increasingly, state and national competitions. When carvers vied for prizes each was supplied with the same amount of packed snow or blocks of ice and expected to create their sculpture within a prescribed time limit. The Winter Carnival often separated amateur from professional ice carvers by the amount of ice they were provided: a block for an amateur compared with twenty blocks each measuring 10 by 20 by 40 inches for the professional sculptor. In 1991 the snow block measured six by ten feet. Teams of three worked for two and a half days in competition for prizes. They received a "tool kit" with a coal shovel, an axe, two snow chisels, water pail, a ladder, and two machetes, but were not allowed to use the power tools an ice sculptor utilized. Ice carving competitions have often been held in Rice Park, while snow sculpture competitions have taken place in Como Park, on the Capitol Mall, and at the John Rose Oval in Roseville.

Sapporo, Japan, celebrates winter with snow sculptures galore. Throughout the city and its parks examples of ephemeral frozen art are on view. Japanese snow sculptors from Sapporo came to St. Paul in 1978. Seven artists turned 600 tons of snow into a scene called "The Battle Between Cho-un and Koken" in Como Park. In 1987 another group of artists came from the Sapporo Snow Festival to create images drawn from Kabuki and Noh theatre traditions. In their sculpture (twenty-four feet high by fifty feet long, by twenty-six feet wide) one mask of a beautiful maiden and another mask of a snake demon were carved and set on either side of a lion dancer. Snowmaking equipment from the Wild Mountain ski resort was used for the snow sculpture on Harriet Island.

Ice carving called "Teamsters of the North" from the 1916 Carnival. Courtesy of the J. J. Hill Library.

1937 postcard displaying a snow sculpture of Ben Hur, by Josef Edlbauer.

tures for Courthouse Square in 1939. For the Victory Carnival of 1946 military figures were carved in ice to place on the Ice Palace parapets. For the 1955 Carnival, standing almost where the 1937 Ice Palace had been, a twenty-four foot tall ice block with Boreas and his Queen was done by Peter Lupori and Daniel Soderlind. Parker Seiler, later a snow palace builder, came from Michigan to create snow sculpture at Como Park. His 1963 effort was a clown.

For the 1989 Carnival ten ice carvers with experience in the Harbin (China) Ice Lantern Festival came to St. Paul. That Festival, held annually since 1981, features ice sculpture in a city park as well as in many other locations. When St. Paul Carnival staff saw a story about the Chinese Festival in the March 1988 issue of *National Geographic* magazine they felt the Chinese carvers should be invited to St. Paul. Thus, an ice dragon came to frosty life in Mears Park.

In 1990, paying tribute to other ice sculpture traditions, Carnival organizers invited a group of seven artists from Sverdlovsk, in Siberia, to carve episodes (especially a firebird) from Russian fairy tales on the Capitol Mall. That was not one of Minnesota's snowiest years so the Tall Snowman which was also planned for the Mall, and expected to set a new record at over seventy feet tall, melted before that goal was reached.

Winter Carnival activities have taken place in many of the city's neighborhoods. For the past ten years, ever since 1993, the Macalester – Groveland community has sponsored a snow sculpture contest on Summit Avenue's median strip, between Albert and Pascal streets. Entrants are assigned a 4 x 4 foot block of snow and are given several hours to shape their sculptures, using shovels and trowels, the usual tools of the snow sculptor.

Corn stalk mazes became popular attractions on Minnesota farms in the 1990s. For the Carnival an ice maze was constructed in Como Park for the first time in 1999 with discarded Christmas trees. The following year walls built of ice blocks from Lake Phalen were shaped into a snowflake. These ice mazes, 200 to 300 feet long snow slides, often built by Army Reserve construction battalions, and the Wilderness Experience or Inquiry have become regular features of the Winter Carnival in Como Park. The Wilderness Experience offers families an opportunity to try snowshoeing, dogsled racing, cross-country skiing, and learn the elements of winter camping, all from expert instructors.

1937 ice sculpture of an Indian Chief. Postcard courtesy of Wally Wescott.

Snow sculpture of a hand holding an American flag, created for the 1991 Carnival by Terry and Jeanne Labelle and Tom Pnewski. Courtesy of the author.

Fish sculpture from the 1984 Winter Carnival.

Once A King, Always A King

3

Several versions exist of the Legend of the Winter Carnival. Each explains the story behind the festival and expands its cast of costumed characters. From the first Winter Carnival of 1886 onward, the major participants have been the King and Queen of the Snows (Borealis or Boreas, and Aurora) and their rival, the Fire King (Ignis or Vulcanus). Over the years other personalities have joined the cast and their names have changed. What is most striking is that anyone who has assumed the identity of King, Queen, Fire King, or any of the other roles tends to remain involved in the work of the Winter Carnival for years afterward. Truly, it becomes "Once a King, Always a King."

In the earliest story, written by J. H. Hanson in "The Crystal Carnival" (1885), Borealis and his queen Aurora Borealis are invited to visit the gorgeous palace of ice. They arrive by train "from the icy caverns of the crystallized region beyond the ken of men." A pageant, parade, and masquerade are organized in their honor and a great magician causes celestial fires to illuminate the palace. The Fire King resents this attention since he wants to rule the kingdom. With his army, the Fire King attacks and is defeated by Borealis, aided by Megissogwan the Magician and the Spirit of the North Wind. For a week all is calm; fetes and festivities fill the fast fleeting hours. But then another army approaches. Fearing more hostilities between the Kings of Summer and Winter, the veterans of the Grand Army of the Republic come to take possession of the palace and arbitrate. The Ice King surrenders and a treaty is negotiated. From now on the "monarchs of the Four Seasons" shall reign in succession. But for the next thirty years a palace of ice shall be built every year for the Ice King's festivities.

Finding individuals to enact the roles of Winter Carnival characters was at first solely the task of the organizing committee. Now, selection committees and officers of the alumni groups may seek out each year's Winter Carnival cast of characters. Individuals apply after finding their own sponsors. Today those interested in becoming Wind Princes, Royal Guards, or Wind Princesses realize that their duties last for a full year, while for members of the Vulcan Krewe it is a five-year obligation. It is as much a commitment as those assumed by the major figures of carnival royalty. Earlier in Winter Carnival history that was not the case. Prior to 1937, Winter Carnival Kings and Queens could put aside their royal robes when the Winter Carnival ended as their ceremonial roles were finished.

Today's Winter Carnival Kings (either Boreas or Vulcanus) are business owners or senior executives, usually married, often of late middle age. They are able to commit both time and funds to their roles. The Queen of the Snows has traditionally been single, in her twenties, and initially

Borealis IV (Charles E. Flandrau) and his Lord High Chamberlain (Samuel Van Sant) in their regal finery, 1896. Courtesy of Steve Nelson.

was usually an employee of her sponsor's firm. In the first Carnival season there were both an Ice King and Queen, and a younger pair known as Prince and Princess Carnival. Borealis I was a retired Civil War general named Richard W. Johnson, who was originally from Kentucky. His first military duty post had been Fort Snelling. After the Civil War he returned to St. Paul in 1870. His Queen was Mrs. Lorenzo L. C. Brooks (*St. Paul Dispatch*, January 30, 1886). Prince Carnival was William Hamm, Sr. His Princess, Marie Dreis Scheffer, was married to the Carnival treasurer, Albert Scheffer. Prince and Princess Carnival presided over the German parade, dressed in the Louis XIV garb of that year. Eight years after their Carnival year, Hamm married the Scheffers' daughter, also named Marie.

KINGS OF WINTER

1886 GENERAL RICHARD W. JOHNSON, Borealis Rex I
1886 WILLIAM HAMM, SR., Prince Carnival
1887 DR. JOHN H. MURPHY, Borealis Rex II
1888 EDWARD W. DURANT, Borealis Rex III

1896 JUSTICE CHARLES E. FLANDRAU, Borealis Rex IV

1916 J. P. ELMER, Boreas Rex I
1917 J. P. RIDLER, Boreas Rex II
1918 J. P. RIDLER, Boreas Rex II

1928 C. H. (JACK) BEVINGTON, King Midway
1929 PASCAL A. BECKJORD, Chief Midway
1930 H. D. RISDON, King Boreas

1937 FRANK L. MADDEN, Boreas Rex III
1938 DR. ERNEST S. POWELL, Boreas Rex IV
1939 CARL R. GRAY, JR., Boreas Rex V
1940 J. L. SHIELY, SR., Boreas Rex VI
1941 JOHN F. SCOTT, SR., Boreas Rex VII
1942 LAMBERT S. GILL, Boreas Rex VIII

1946 THOMAS J. GIBBONS, Boreas Rex IX
1947 R. E. ALBRECHT, Boreas Rex X
1948 EDWARD C. HAMPE, Boreas Rex XI

1949	CLARENCE A. MALEY, Boreas Rex XII
1950	NORMAN H. NELSON, Boreas Rex XIV
1951	HENRY J. MICHEL, Boreas Rex XV
1952	A. LEE RUNYON, Boreas Rex XVI
1953	J. RUSSELL SWEITZER, Boreas Rex XVII
1954	WALTER V. DORLE, Boreas Rex XVIII
1955	JOSEPH A. ROGERS, Boreas Rex XIX
1956	WALLACE L. BOSS, Boreas Rex XX
1957	JAMES F. OWENS, JR., Boreas Rex XXI
1958	ROHLAND H. THOMSSEN, SR., Boreas Rex XXII
1959	H. E. SCHELL, Boreas Rex XXIII
1960	FRED A. SODERBERG, Boreas Rex XXIV
1961	JOHN D. MCGOWAN, Boreas Rex XXV
1962	WESLEY M. (BUD) CHANDLER, Boreas Rex XVI
1963	HENRI G. FOUSSARD, Boreas Rex XXVII
1964	RUSSELL M. JOHNSON, Boreas Rex XXVIII
1965	LAWRENCE W. THULIN, Boreas Rex XXIX
1966	GEORGE J. RUTMAN, Boreas Rex XXX
1967	WILLIAM POPPENBERGER, Boreas Rex XXI
1968	EMIL JANDRIC, Boreas Rex XXXII
1969	JOHN H. DONOHUE, III, Boreas Rex XXXIII
1970	WILLIAM H. HITE, Boreas Rex XXXIV
1971	FREDERICK BJORKLUND, Boreas Rex XXXV
1972	ROBERT O. ASHBACH, Boreas Rex XXXVI
1973	A. L. MUELLER, Boreas Rex XXXVII
1974	ROY M. SVEE, Boreas Rex XXXVIII
1975	RICHARD J. LONG, Boreas Rex XXXIX
1976	C. DONALD RIECK, Boreas Rex XL
1977	MARVIN ELLISON, Boreas Rex XLI
1978	DANIEL F. DOLAN, Boreas Rex XLII
1979	ROBERT CARTER, SR., Boreas Rex XLIII
1980	NORMAN MEARS, Boreas Rex XLIV
1981	RICHARD SCHAAK, Boreas Rex XLV
1982	VICTOR P. REIM, JR., Boreas Rex XLVI
1983	CHARLES HALL, Boreas Rex XLVII
1984	DONALD LARSON, Boreas Rex XLVIII
1985	JOHN A. FISHER, Boreas Rex XLIX
1986	JERRY CRARY, Boreas Rex L
1987	TED STEICHEN, Boreas Rex LI
1988	DICK ZEHRING, Boreas Rex LII
1989	RICHARD BARBARI, Boreas Rex LIII
1990	LOU COLLETTE, Boreas Rex LIV
1991	GIL THOELE, Boreas Rex LV
1992	BUD ROONEY, Boreas Rex LVI
1993	TOM HUPPERT, Boreas Rex LVII
1994	TED ZWIEG, Boreas Rex LVIII
1995	LES MALMQUIST, Boreas Rex LIX
1996	TOM BRAMWELL, Boreas Rex LX
1997	DAN OLSON, Boreas Rex LXI
1998	PHIL JUNGWIRTH, Boreas Rex LXII
1999	PAT MCCULLOUGH, Boreas Rex LXIII
2000	GARY HAIDER, Boreas Rex LXIV
2001	GREG KUNTZ, Boreas Rex LXV
2002	TIM MADDEN, Boreas Rex LXVI
2003	DICK KEDROWSKI, Boreas Rex LXVII

Beginning his reign, Borealis I arrived at city hall in his special sleigh to request the keys to the city, both of them in fact, one labeled "front entrance" and the other, "rear entrance." Mayor Edmund Rice welcomed the King, gave him the keys and a scroll listing the City's officers, and then made several requests, stating:

> The blind pig [an unlicensed saloon] has made a disgraceful effort to gain a footing in our city. Please freeze him out. Also, please make all citizens and non-resident lot owners remove the snow from the sidewalks fronting their property.

And, Rice hoped, that the king could compel the city comptroller to print his delinquent financial reports. The King promised to root out the pig and have the comptroller submit his reports (*St. Paul Daily Globe*, February 3, 1886). Then he and his entourage went on to the Ice Palace.

In 1887 no Queen was selected, but the next year the Queen of the Snows was the daughter of St. Paul's long-serving mayor, Robert Smith. The mayor of Minneapolis, Albert Ames, served as the second Fire King Coal. And then, after several years without carnivals, came 1896. Retired Minnesota Supreme Court Justice Charles E. Flandrau, who looked most venerable with a long white beard, shared his throne with Andrew

Heckler, who was employed at the Sterling wine shop. The ample Mr. Heckler, dubbed "Gloriana, the Daisy Queen," was said to represent the "New Woman," an idea that was just coming into discussion. The New Woman sought a larger role in society through education, leading to careers and the vote for women. Gloriana wore a large hat "of indescribable shape," which the King wrote was "something simply splendid; it did not begin and never ended," a Dolly Varden blouse with balloon sleeves ("terrible space consumers," wrote Borealis, "only equalled by your bloomers"), colored bloomers, and checkered spats over her shoes. Rather than appearing with Borealis on his float, the independent-minded Queen rode astride a Percheron pony in the parade. When they reached City Hall Borealis received a large gilded key of welcome. He accepted the key as a token of his rule over St. Paul, and then proclaimed:

> We abolish all taxes and agreements
> We declare all debts, great and small, paid and
>   extinguished.
> We liberate all prisoners.
> We declare the sick well, the poor rich, and
>   reduce the price of all drinks to 5 cents.
> Let everybody henceforth be happy.

Gloriana immediately claimed the key as her property, expressing the fear that if his majesty had charge of it, her majesty would have to sit up nights waiting for him to come home. In "his most chivalrous manner," Mayor Smith quickly surrendered the key to the Daisy Queen (*St. Paul Dispatch*, January 22, 1896).

Due to warm weather and a lack of funding it would be twenty years before another king or queen rode through the streets of St. Paul.

In 1916 a committee of businessmen decided St. Paul needed another Carnival, to be referred to as the Outdoor Sports Carnival, rather than as a "Winter" Carnival. As the manager of the Carnival wrote to the editors of the St. Paul newspapers before the next Carnival, it was feared that otherwise "thousands of people over the country would get an erroneous impression regarding the climate and the country itself in the Northwest if we called it the Winter Carnival" (Letter of H. P. Wickham to editors Vance, Galt, Briggs, and Bowers, September 29, 1916, SPOSA, MHS). With Louis W. Hill, Sr., of the Northern Pacific Railroad as president, the Carnival committee determined to "Make it a Hot One." Once more it was an idea with great appeal.

QUEENS OF THE SNOWS

1886	MRS. LORENZO L. C. BROOKS
1886	MARIE DREIS SCHEFFER, Princess Carnival
1887	No queen selected
1888	MINA SMITH
1896	ANDREW HECKLER, "Gloriana" the Daisy Queen
1916	108 queens reigned
1916	IRENE GRAYSTON, Carnival Girl
1917	ELSIE CARLSON, HELEN GROGAN, & LILLIAN SMABY
1917	MABEL LOOBY, Carnival Girl
1918	MABEL LOOBY, Carnival Girl
1922	ANNA CHRISTIE, Queen of Queens
1928	EDNA M. BOLKE, Queen Midway
1929	HELEN WEBB, Queen Midway
1930	LEE HALLERAN, Queen Snowdrop
1937	GRETCHEN HAUENSTEIN WOLFE
1938	MARION O'HARA
1939	IRENE FOSS UNDERWOOD
1940	MARY LOU MCDONNELL SCHNEEWEISS

1941	KATHLEEN HANSON NICKELSON
1942	MARTHA DUPUIS BENKE
1943	GRACE TALBOT, Miss Freedom
1946	SHIRLEY PETERSON GRAIZIGER
1947	HELEN DUFFY MURPHY
1948	MAXINE EMERSON JENSEN
1948	BETTY JOHNSON JOHNSON
1949	JOAN SCHALLER HANSON
1950	MARY KAY LEMIRE LUKOSKIE
1951	AUDREY SHEAHAN SAGER
1952	BEVERLY PRAZAK BIAGI
1953	CAROLE RAE O'GARY DRURY
1954	MARY LOU LIPKE OLSON
1955	DOROTHY ARNEBERG FURLONG
1956	MARYLEE SWAN MAIDA
1957	EVA WICKER GALLAGHER
1957	BARBARA GEIGER DONNAN
1958	SALLY SHIELDS POFERI
1959	KAREN SONTAG SATTEL
1960	MURIEL LUX SCHLITGEN
1961	MARY ANN SCHWAB WETOSKA
1962	PENNY HICKS WIGGINS
1963	ROBERTA ANNIBAS ZADRA
1964	CARRIE PATCH SAMPLE
1965	CARLA AUGST LEVANDER
1966	JEANNE WILLIAMS RISLOVE
1967	ANGELINE JOHNSON CARLSON
1968	BARBARA STROBUSH KEENAN
1969	MARY LAFOND MEDVED
1970	MARILYN KOPPY DAVERN
1971	CHARLOTTE LAMPE SEEP
1972	ANDREA AUGE PAIST
1973	CHRISTINE O'CONNOR ZAK
1974	REBECCA STOCKING BROWN
1975	BOBBIE MISCHKE FLANAGAN
1976	DEBRA MICHELS MCFERRON
1977	MICHELLE RAFFERTY
1978	MARLENE RICHTER KILLA
1979	KRISTINE HANSON FINHOLT STEARLEY
1980	MARGARET ARNEBERG MANDERFELD
1981	LINDA GRANT LYNCH
1982	JACQUIE SAMUEL EMMER
1983	BETH ACHTERLING NAUGHTON
1984	SHARI BONFE RANTZ
1985	TORREY HOLMEN ASP
1986	SUSAN IVANCIE
1987	SANDRA SWENSON

1988	LAURIE HAMMOND WIENMEYER
1989	KATHRYN ARKO REIFENBURGER
1990	JILL MUELLER ELDRIDGE
1991	LISA LANG
1992	CHRISTINA PROFT SCHWIETZ
1993	JULIE WARD JOHNSTON
1994	JOYCE LACEY
1995	KIM JUNG JA KANTOROWICZ SCHILLING
1996	MAUREEN DAMMAN
1997	KARI BOE SCHMIDTZ
1998	DANIELLE RADKE
1999	MARTHA HILL
2000	JULIETTE SPIER
2001	MISTY ENGLER MCGOWAN
2002	JENNIFER HEYING
2003	AMANDA LYN MELQUIST

In the roster of Carnival royalty the four Borealises of the nineteenth century were succeeded in 1916 by the first Boreas. The Fire King Coals I through IV were followed by Ignis Rex (later renamed Vulcan and then Vulcanus Rex). In 1916 the committee selected the male royals, but decided on another method for choosing the queen. Each of the numerous marching clubs, representing local businesses and schools, was invited to select a queen. As Louis Hill told the Dayton's Bluff Commercial Club, the queen would not be selected from Summit Avenue, but from one of the factories or institutions in the city (*St. Paul Pioneer Press*, January 11, 1916).

The Business and Professional Men's Marching Club could not decide on a candidate so the nine-month old daughter of their president was selected. Natalie Lethert Ayers, known as the "Baby Queen," would say in later years that not only was she the youngest, but in 1937 she was also chosen as a lady-in-waiting, as

The storming of the Ice Palace is led by Fire King Coal under the rockets' red glare. Cartoon by George Rehse, St. Paul Daily Globe *(January 25, 1896).*

the princesses were then called. Then she would mention an added distinction. At a party for Carnival royalty at the Louis W. Hill home Boreas bounced the Baby Queen on his lap, causing her to burp loudly. That, she said, was a distinction that no other queen would ever have.

Boreas was asked to make the final choice, but he declared himself unable to decide. As a result he presented each with a small box holding a crown, and all 108 ladies presided over Carnival events as Queen. In *The Deluxe Souvenir View Book* (Carnival Publishing Company, St. Paul, 1916) individual photographs appear of the queens, but identification is only given for their sponsors.

George Wood fastens the skis of the Carnival Girl (Irene Grayston) at the Town and Country Club, 1916. Courtesy of Eugene DiMartino.

Perhaps the most photographed woman of the Carnival was not a queen at all. She was the Carnival Girl. Irene Grayston, wearing a red coat trimmed in fur, appeared on postcards, posters, buttons, poster stamps, menu covers, sheet music, cigar wrappers, and on a sack for "Carnival Girl Flour" from Capital City Milling Company of St. Paul. The executive committee of the St. Paul Outdoor Sports Carnival Association rejected a request from a distiller to use the Carnival Girl image on his whiskey bottle labels. Stories about the Carnival Girl were widely published and a contest was organized by the *St. Paul Dispatch and Pioneer Press* for the best likeness of her. Sketches and paintings entered were displayed in the windows of the Golden Rule department store. As the best known lady in the pageant, the Carnival Girl entered the Grand Ball on the arm of the Ice King.

After the Carnival ended, the queens hosted a luncheon for Louis W. Hill where he was presented with a silver loving cup in thanks for all of his efforts. This cup is now a part of the collection of the St. Paul Festival and Heritage Foundation. Hill responded with a verse paraphrased from François Villon's poem:

Alas for the Queens! For one by one
The wind has blown them all away,
The young and the fair, in the midst of their fun,
O, where are the Queens of Yesterday?

And then Hill added: "Wait another year."
(St. Paul Pioneer Press, *February 13, 1916*).

The next year another Carnival Girl was selected to pose for all of the advance publicity since Miss Grayston had married. Mabel Looby was shown in a blue fur trimmed coat, soaring on skis. In some of the posters the 1916 Carnival Girl skates just behind her, like a ghost from the past.

Seeking to avoid 1916's contretemps over the queen, the 1917 Winter Carnival committee asked three of the finalists in the dogsled race from Winnipeg to St. Paul to decide the winner. But the racers could not agree so there were three Queens for 1917. It was the Carnival Girl, however, who shared the stage with Boreas II at the coronation.

Although there was some thought of continuing the Winter Carnival in 1918, America's entry into the Great War effectively ended any such plans. A one-day sports festival was held at Fort Snelling in 1918, with the 1917 Carnival royalty present. The new queen bore the title "Miss Freedom." Officially no further Winter Carnivals took place until 1937, but that is not quite accurate. The city of St. Paul, rather than its business community, organized a Winter Sports Carnival in 1922, and in so doing perhaps set a record. The *St. Paul Dispatch and Pioneer Press* sponsored a beauty pageant. Girls could enter by neighborhoods (Phalen, Como, West End, Tri-Park and Riverview) and a "committee of artists" selected the Queen of Queens. Anna Christie, who won the contest, triumphed over a field of 800 entrants.

Six years later the Midway Civic Club organized the first of what would be three Winter Carnivals, complete with parades, sports, races, an ice palace, and the appropriate royalty. In 1929 the Midway queen candidates represented the twelve districts within Midway. Helen Webb was named Queen Midway, but rather than a tiara she wore a feather since that Carnival had an Indian theme.

The Queens, Hussars, Boreas II (J. P. Ridder) and the Carnival Girl (Marie Looby) at the Coronation ceremony, 1917.

KINGS OF FIRE

1886 DELOS A. MONFORT, Fire King Coal I
1887 DR. ALBERT A. AMES, Fire King Coal II
1888 SEN. DANIEL A. MORRISON, Fire King Coal III

1896 WILLIAM H. EUSTIS, Fire King Coal IV

1916 RONALD STEWART, Ignis Rex, Vulcan Rex I
1917 JAMES HEALEY, Prince Paul, Vulcan Rex II

1937 GUSTAV C. AXELROD, Vulcan Rex III
1938 W. LUKE CRAWFORD, Vulcan Rex IV
1939 ADOLPH E. GIERE, Vulcan Rex V
1940 E. R. REIFF, Vulcan Rex VI
1941 ADOLPH BREMER, JR., Vulcan Rex VII
1942 EDWARD W. BERGSTROM, Vulcan Rex VIII

1946 GEORGE SCHRANTZ, Vulcan Rex IX
1947 A. J. BRIOSCHI, Vulcan Rex X
1948 GEORGE L. HELENIAK, Vulcan Rex XI
1949 E. J. JEFFERS, Vulcan Rex XII
1950 WILLIAM G. KLETT, Vulcan Rex XIII
1951 S. A. BERTELSEN, Vulcan Rex XIV
1952 LAURENCE K. HODGSON, Vulcan Rex XV
1953 WILLIAM S. LUND, Vulcan Rex XVI
1954 JAMES C. SCHMIDT, Vulcan Rex XVII
1955 JAMES F. SHIELY, Vulcan Rex XVIII
1956 PETER S. POPOVICH, Vulcan Rex XIX
1957 J. PERRY DOTSON, Vulcan Rex XX
1958 WILFRED S. SCHLAEFER, Vulcan Rex XXI
1959 JOHN A. WORKS, Vulcan Rex XXII
1960 DANIEL R. BAKER, Vulcan Rex XXIII
1961 ROBERT LAWRENCE, Vulcan Rex XXIV
1962 FRANK OBERG, Vulcan Rex XXV
1963 DICK ROSACKER, Vulcan Rex XXVI
1964 STEVE ZOBEL, Vulcan Rex XXVII
1965 DON BOEHMER, Vulcanus Rex XXVIII
1966 BOB THIERS, Vulcanus Rex XXIX
1967 DICK HASSETT, Vulcanus Rex XXX
1968 HOWARD CHRISTENSEN, Vulcanus Rex XXXI
1969 RAY NEUENFELDT, Vulcanus Rex XXXII
1970 JOE ROGERS, Vulcanus Rex XXXIII
1971 BOB FLAKNE, Vulcanus Rex XXXIV
1972 ROGER SORENSEN, Vulcanus Rex XXXV
1973 JOE SHIELDS, Vulcanus Rex XXXVI
1974 LYLE LACKNER, Vulcanus Rex XXXVII
1975 RALPH NARDINI, Vulcanus Rex XXXVIII
1976 PETER LARAMY, Vulcanus Rex XXXIX
1977 JACK CRAWFORD, Vulcanus Rex XL
1978 JOHN BRADNER SMITH, Vulcanus Rex XLI

1979 TOM BECKEN, Vulcanus Rex XLII
1980 R. F. (RED) ROBERTS, Vulcanus Rex XLIII
1981 CHARLIE ROSENBERGER, Vulcanus Rex XLIV
1982 IVAN WEISS, Vulcanus Rex XLV
1983 DAN SHIELY, Vulcanus Rex XLVI
1984 ED ALTERMATT, Vulcanus Rex XLVII
1985 STEPHEN P. POPOVICH, Vulcanus Rex XLVIII
1986 JAY SALMEN, Vulcanus Rex XLIX
1987 CHUCK MASTEL, Vulcanus Rex L
1988 ROGER PULKRABEK, Vulcanus Rex LI
1989 MARVIN LEVINE, Vulcanus Rex LII
1990 BILL SANDISON, Vulcanus Rex LIII
1991 JOHN ZOBEL, Vulcanus Rex LIV
1992 TERRY FENELON, Vulcanus Rex LV
1993 GERALD E. LANAHAN, Vulcanus Rex LVI
1994 GARY HILL, Vulcanus Rex LVII
1995 TOM PNEWSKI, Vulcanus Rex LVIII
1996 HOWIE REGISTER, Vulcanus Rex LIX
1997 JACQUES PEULEN, Vulcanus Rex LX
1998 WALLY ROSSINI, Vulcanus Rex LXI
1999 BOYD BOWMAN, Vulcanus Rex LXII
2000 MARK J. SALMEN, Vulcanus Rex LXIII
2001 DANIEL SCHULTZ, Vulcanus Rex LXIV
2002 LARRY MAHONEY, Vulcanus Rex LXV
2003 JIM EGGERT, Vulcanus Rex LXVI

As the Great Depression neared its end, a new group of St. Paul businessmen determined to revive the Winter Carnival. The St. Paul Winter Carnival Association brought back the palaces and parades, but changed elements of the basic story and its presentation. Then came World War II. When it ended a new group took charge of the city's festival. The Saintpaulites, as they called the new organization, organized Winter Carnivals from 1946 (The "Victory" Carnival) until 1959. The next sponsoring organization was the St. Paul Winter Carnival Association, which in turn was succeeded in 1993 by the St. Paul Festival and Heritage Foundation.

Rewriting the legend was the task undertaken by the third Boreas Rex, Frank L. Madden, a columnist for the *St. Paul Dispatch*. In *The Rollicking Realm of Boreas* (1941) he expands and explains the Carnival traditions with their Greek, Roman, and English royal influences. In Greek mythology Boreas and his three brothers were in charge of the winds. Boreas controlled the blustery yet healthy North Wind, Euros the East, to Notos went the South and to Zephryus the West. The brothers all "cavorted gaily over the land and sea, spreading fogs, chasing clouds, whipping rains, scattering mists . . ." until one starry night Boreas skimmed over "a winter paradise known to men as Minnesota." The seven hills of St. Paul sparkled bewitchingly under a blanket of snow. Boreas immediately decided to make Saint Paul the capital city of all his dominions "and the winter playground of Boreas." Older gods approved and suggested celebrating with a Carnival to last for ten scintillating days and brilliant nights. Parades, receptions in the Great Hall of Jupiter, and athletic contests (especially a great curling match, or bonspiel) crowded the days of Carnival. But there was envy and danger approaching as Vulcan, the Fire King, fumed and paced in the dark recesses of Carver's Cave.

As the people marched, sang and enjoyed feats of great daring Boreas announced that a Great Ball would soon take place. There he would select the most beautiful of all the maidens to join him as the Queen of the Snows. After the glittering ball word reached Boreas of a plot. Vulcan planned to storm the Ice Palace. Boreas quickly ordered his guards to capture the Fire King. Vulcan was captured near the shores of White Bear Lake, but escaped, aided by the treachery of Euros and Notos. A mighty assault was then launched on Boreas' Ice Palace by Vulcan. Boreas wanted to resist, but the Queen of the Snows advised him to yield. She said that the people had enjoyed the promised ten days of Carnival. Now it was time for them to return to work and for

Frank Madden's booklet provides the Carnival with its basic legend.

"An ideal place," exulted Boreas. "I will make Saint Paul the capital city of all, my dominions – it will henceforth be emblazoned to the world as the winter playground of the realm of Boreas."

~ Frank L. Madden, *The Rollicking Realm of Boreas – A Legend* (1937).

Boreas to leave his winter capital and return to the home of the gods on Olympus. Thus ended Frank Madden's delightful version of the Winter Carnival legend.

New to the Carnival in Madden's version of the legend were the three Wind Princes. They would be distinguished in years to come through costumes and hats. Euros, the East Wind, usually wears a turban, vest and baggy, Mid-eastern pants, while his boot tips curl upwards. Zephyrus wears cowboy garb with hat and boots, and Notos dons headgear to suit his Mexican charro outfit. Also present in Madden's telling were the ladies-in-

waiting of the Queen of the Snows. Later they would be renamed "wind princesses" and assigned to the territories of Notos, Euros, and Zephyrus. Titan (a second North Wind) was at first a lesser cousin to Boreas, but in 1960 was revealed as a brother of the Ice King. His costume is a frosty white for his suit and hat, but his boots are traditionally silver. Persons who take on the role of a Prince of the Wind are usually active members of business associations in those neighborhoods which they represent. The buttons each Wind Prince hands out usually identify both the prince and his commercial affiliation.

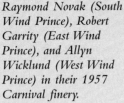

Raymond Novak (South Wind Prince), Robert Garrity (East Wind Prince), and Allyn Wicklund (West Wind Prince) in their 1957 Carnival finery.

WEST WINDS AND PRINCESSES

1940	PATRICK TOWLE
1941	FRANK RING
1942	LEONARD MCNEIL
1946	WALTER KJELSON
1947	FRANK MONDIKE
1948	HAROLD MORK
1949	JOE ROGERS
1950	CHARLES T. KENNY
1951	MAX HOUTS
1952	FRED SAAM
1953	REUBEN SWANSON
1954	NORMAN NELSON – JOANN KIMMEL
1955	WALTER F. RIHM
1956	WALTER BECHIK
1957	ALLYN B. WICKLUND
1958	F. A. AMUNDSEN
1959	ORRIN STONE
1960	ROBERT BRATNOBER
1961	RICHARD STEENBERG
1962	HAROLD B. SHAPIRO
1963	DWIGHT E. MARRIOTT – MARY SCHWEITZ
1964	KENNETH I. TREPP
1965	BRUCE F. JOHNSTON
1966	LEROY DREW
1967	DONALD ZALK
1968	RUSSELL SWANSON
1969	JOHN F. ROONEY – MARNIE LENTSCH
1970	LOWERY SMITH – CAROL THOMPSON

1971	FRANK COLLETTI – GLORIA VANNELLI
1972	MONTY KRONSTEDT
1973	C. DONALD RIECK – PATRICIA FALLON
1974	JOSEPH C. ARRIGONI, SR. – MICHELLE COLLETTI
1975	JAN L. JANSEN – VICTORIA HILTON
1976	PETE PAULOS – MARY JO BORTZ
1977	BILL OMAN – DEE HAMMOND
1978	CLAUDE ANDERSON – SANDRA FENNER
1979	STEVE C. BILLINGS – SUSAN VAN HOEF
1980	DONOVAN J. FISHER – MARY MADLAND
1981	THOMAS PARRISH – KATHLEEN DUFFY
1982	GARY SVOBODA – STACEE ANN CARDENAS
1983	BILL NIELSEN – KATHLEEN BOEHM
1984	CARLTON HOLERUD – TERESA LUTHER / MARY MADDEN
1985	RON LARSEN – JOLENE REINHARDT
1986	ROGER A. BONFE – LONI LAU
1987	RICHARD A. KRUSE – MINDI RUMPCA
1988	LEN CARLSON – JILL SCZEPANSKI
1989	DON CRAIGHEAD – ANNE JUNGWIRTH
1990	THOMAS G. FENNER - MICHELLE DILL
1991	CHUCK MCCANN – JULIE PETERSON
1992	BILL BURG – WENDY RIPPBURGER
1993	RICHARD PELLOW – AMY FELLEGY
1994	VERN RIEDIGER – MEGAN REED
1995	EARL SMITH – TIFFANY WELLS
1996	DAVE THUNE – DIANE HOPEN
1997	JERRY SHOWALTER – SHERRY ENGEL
1998	MIKE STONE – CATHRYN DAVIDSON
1999	MARK CHAPPLE – ERICA HALTER
2000	MIKE JAY – MOLLY DAVERN
2001	ROY MEIXELL – ELIN SCHOENFELDER
2002	RENNIE SMITH – KERI ABEL
2003	SCOTT TOUSIGNANT – ERIN GEBHART

SOUTH WINDS AND PRINCESSES

1940	BRADLEY MAHANA
1941	A. J. BRIOSCHI
1942	MILTON R. FLEU
1946	EDWARD DEVITT
1947	JOHN SEEGER
1948	VAL BLAQUE
1949	JOHN VERSTRAETE
1950	LOUIS VILLAUME, JR.
1951	RAYMOND H. HENSE
1952	GORDON DAVIS
1953	EDWIN C. JERABEK
1954	RALPH PETERS

1955	ROBERT DAVIS
1956	JACK STUHLMAN
1957	RAY NOVAK
1958	JOSEPH I. "JOE" KRAMER
1959	JOE STEVENS
1960	HOWARD "HOWIE" RUNGE
1961	FRANK MEGA
1962	PETER "PETE" MANSUR
1963	ORVILLE "ORV" BRINK
1964	ROBERT "BOB" CARTER, SR.
1965	ALLEN "AL" LINDBERG
1966	TOM WALLACE
1967	HOWARD "HOWIE" SCHLETZ
1968	RONALD "RON" MERGENS – JANET OSIECKI
1969	JAMES E. "JIM" PETERS – JACKIE BLACK
1970	WALTER "WALLY" NELSON – MARY SUNDBERG
1971	HARLAN HENDRICKS - MARY GERVAIS
1972	BERNARD HUSNIK
1973	HAROLD C. "SWEDE" SWANSON – GAIL ANDERSON
1974	HAROLD "HAP" LEVANDER – MARY GRAIZIGER
1975	FORREST GLEWWE – TERESA RADABAUGH
1976	ROBERT "BOB" CARTER, JR. – RENEE FEIDT
1977	WILLIAM "BILL" BARTL – LAURA TREPANIER
1978	STEVE LOEDING – MICHELE ROGERS
1979	SID DAILY – LISA DANIELSON
1980	VIC WENZEL – LYNN ANDERSON
1981	J. ROBERT STASSEN – DIANE DOLAN
1982	CHUCK LINNEROOTH – ROXANNE RADMER
1983	JOE SCHAEFFER – COLLEEN STAHMER
1984	MACKENZIE R. "BUTCH" CANNIFF – CHARLOTTE SYME
1985	P. JAMES TAURINSKAS – TINA BULACH
1986	TIM BUCHHOLZ – PAIGE WALLIN
1987	TOM RICKER – LORI O'MALLEY
1988	WILLIAM J. HOCKING – ANGELA DELMONT
1989	MIKE WENDEL – MARY CORBO
1990	JOHN BENNETT – CINDY HAEHNEL
1991	KEVIN LEARY – CLAIRE FRIEDMANN
1992	MARK LINDELL – CELESTE JAEGER
1993	STEVE SNELLING – MARY LOUISE KEMP
1994	TOM LEONARD – NICKY MEAD
1995	JERRY GUNDERMAN – MAUREEN SCHULTE-WIRRER
1996	GREG KUNTZ – JOAN FISH
1997	JEFF BOCHE – LAURA BLAISDELL
1998	KEVIN KLIETHERMES – KAREN JOHNSON
1999	JIM KALKAS – FELICE HARPER
2000	JOE GLASS – CHERYL PITTELKOW
2001	MATTHEW WALLACE – GENA JOHNSTON
2002	TROY MOSER – CARRIE BETH DAVIDSON
2003	STEVE CORTINAS – AIMEE OLSON

NORTH WINDS AND PRINCESSES

1960	JAMES E. WEYANT
1961	WILLIAM LAWRENCE, JR.
1962	GEORGE W. NELSON
1963	DANIEL MUNTEAN
1964	LOUIS SCHIAVINO – MARY MILLS
1965	DON ESCH
1966	EDWARD NOVAK
1967	DON STECHER
1968	DUTCH DELMONTE
1969	EDMUND HAMERNICK
1970	FRANK SCHNEIDER
1971	TOM HUPPERT
1972	JAMES BRADSHAW
1973	MILFORD TOBIN – MARCIA MELANN
1974	EUGENE FASCIANA – GEORGETTE ORMSBY
1975	GLEN L. KLOSKIN – COLLEEN SHIELDS
1976	SAL LOBAIDO – TERESA LUTHER
1977	LEONARD "RED" VANEK – CINDY ANDREOTTI
1978	NORMAN C. HORTON, JR. – DIANE BRINDLEY
1979	DAN A. JEANS – JEANANN WISEMAN
1980	DAVID HOWE – JULIE ARONSON
1981	FRED J. KELLER – NANCY MAHOWALD
1982	CHESTER SCHOENROCK – TAMMY LYMAN
1983	CHARLES GODBOUT – KARI LAW
1984	TED STEICHEN – DEBRA RICHARD
1985	DONALD HUOT – SANDY ROBERTO
1986	GREG M. SHEEHAN – LAURI LAU
1987	ED COLLOVA – MARY JANE THIBAULT
1988	JOSEPH W. NELSON – JACKIE VIDRICK
1989	EDDIE HAMERNICK – LYNN SCHUETZE
1990	ROB LINDER – JODY PETERSON
1991	LLOYD BERGUM – KELLEY MCGOWAN
1992	DENNIS PRCHAL – JEANNE WRICH
1993	TIM SAGER – DANAE WANLESS
1994	LARRY HAUBRICH – SHAWN MARIE TESTER
1995	ERV GRULKOWSKI – SHERRY WALLRICH
1996	DARRIN JOHNSON – KIMBERLY POLLEY
1997	STEVE SCHMIDT – CHRISTINA GROSHENS
1998	RICHARD KEDROWSKI – MARJIE KAISER
1999	PAUL KAMP – CINDY SHANLEY
2000	JAMES LONG – KEELII MONIQUE MCCARTHY
2001	BILL SCHORN – TERI EDSTROM
2002	ERNIE SCHROEDER, JR. – NANCY WURM
2003	MICHAEL LONG – LAUREN QUINTUS

EAST WINDS AND PRINCESSES

1940	RUSSELL HERSETH
1941	RAYMOND M. SCHLICK
1942	JAMES B. SIMONS
1946	CLINTON REDLAND
1947	ELMER GESKE
1948	FRANK TRACY
1949	HARRY MUMSON
1950	EMIL F. CEDARHOLM
1951	WALLY BLOOMQUIST
1952	MATT MORRELLI
1953	DICK SCHWEITZ
1954	RUSSELL CARLSTROM
1955	ARTHUR E. REHNBERG
1956	WARREN HINZE
1957	BOB GARRITY
1958	GERALD C. HEGLAND
1959	KEN BRINDLEY
1960	HARRY BRUCKER
1961	DON JOHNSON – JANET CHAPPLE
1962	WARREN SCHABER
1963	VAN HARWOOD – SANDRA THOMPSON
1964	BOB LEAFGREN
1965	SIG SWANSON
1966	BOB LONDIN
1967	RUSS BOOGREN
1968	ROD JOHNSON – PAT SCHULTZ
1969	HAROLD ANDERSEN – JACKIE BLACK / MICHELLE TWELLS
1970	BOB SHEILD – ALAYNA CARLSON
1971	AL PALM – LINDA AMUNDSON
1972	TOM BEIGLE
1973	JAMES BERGMAN – MARY ANN LYSTAD
1974	JOE CHENOWETH – DAWN BAILEY
1975	PAT MCCULLOUGH – ROBERTA PANNAMANN
1976	ROBERT I. HALL – DEBI YOUNG
1977	WILLIAM "BILL" GODWIN – TEKLA DZENOWAGIS
1978	JERRY EKBLAD – PAMELA DRIVER
1979	SAM BONGIOVANNI – DENISE BAKKE
1980	DON LARSON – CHERY WALLEK
1981	MERLIN HELGEMOE – KATHY JO DUBBS
1982	GREG WULFF – KATHY FLACKEY
1983	RICHARD PETERSON – NANCY HERTOG
1984	GARY BERGREN – SUSAN MCGRATH
1985	STEVE SCHUMACHER – DIANNE KIRST
1986	BOB SNEEN – PAULA REYNOLDS
1987	STEVE KATAINEN – MARIE HOLMEN
1988	TOM STUMPF – JULIANNE FALZONE

1989 RICHARD MCCARTHY – LISA MARIE GOSSELIN
1990 GREG AUGE – LAURA KAINZ
1991 KIM ZARBINSKI – THERESA HUYNH
1992 BOB TUERK – SUSAN PICHA
1993 KEITH VENBURG – ANGELLA GIBSON
1994 STEVE SWAFFORD – JESSICA COLESTOCK
1995 LARRY LAUGHLIN – CINDY SORINI
1996 TERRY FURLONG – SHANNON GORDHAMMER
1997 LONNY PICHE – AMY LINDROTH
1998 RON GRITZMAKER – DEBBIE SEIBERLICH
1999 TOM TUFT – KELLY WARNER
2000 DRAKE ANDERSON – LINDA JAMES
2001 MIKE HAFNER – STACY WEISS
2002 DICK MCCARTHY – JULIA LEPISTO
2003 TOM MEYER – JANNA LARSON

The 1941 Krewe rode an Ahrens-Fox fire truck. Vulcan Rex VII (Adolph Bremer, Jr.) leads the way. Courtesy of Gloria Hicks.

Fire King Coal has been Boreas' nemesis since the beginning of the Carnival. His name changed to Ignis Rex (1916), Vulcan Rex (1937) and finally to Vulcanus Rex in 1965. His role has always been that of a mischief-making rebel whose antics liven the pageantry.

At first only aided by the perfidious Winds in Frank Madden's story, Vulcan was to gain a Krewe of red-suited helpers in 1940. (His predecessors, like Ignis Rex, had to recruit their attack force from the St. Paul Athletic Club's drum and bugle corps.) The Vulcan name came from that of the Roman god of the forge, but in Carnival lore he descends into other fires and emerges with a devilish cohort of seven friends: Baron Hot Sparkus, the Prince of Soot, Count of Ashes, Count Embrious, the Duke of Klinker, General Flameous, and the Grand Duke Fertilious. One of the seven will serve as his Prime Minister as well. All of these titles (except the Prince of Soot whose title was added by Joe Rogers, Vulcanus Rex XXXIII, in 1970) and the red and black costumes were invented by Ernie Reiff, Vulcan Rex VI in 1940, and his wife. The titles are assigned to Krewe members each year by the Fire King.

All of the Queens from the 1916 Outdoor Sports Carnival appear on this advertising card. Courtesy of the J. J. Hill Library.

The Vulcans ride fire trucks in parades and on their runs. For many years they rode on a 1917 model Ahrens-Fox fire truck. Fire trucks, said John Meyers, former Vulcan historian, are never washed during the Winter Carnival. Thus they will look like they have been through a war (or a castle attack). Vulcans especially treasure a vintage truck built in 1932 in Luverne, Minnesota. In May 2002 members of Fire and Brimstone returned to Luverne to celebrate the fire engine's 70th birthday. Several Vulcan Krewes have purchased their own fire trucks. The front doors of the trucks are painted with the Vulcan button design from their particular year. Vulcanus and his Krewe are properly greeted with the salutation: "Hail the Vulc!"

Vulcanus is accompanied by his Krewe, one of whom serves as his principal aide just as the Prime Minister assists Boreas. In recent years

A Vulcan tests his sword on a wall of ice, circa 1946. Photograph by Philip C. Dittes.

Klondike Kates have found perches on the Fire and Brimstone trucks, but in the past Vulcanus actually had a consort. Several dozen Fire Queens, elected in various Minnesota communities, vied for the honor of being Vulcan's queen in 1947. Donna Root of Redwood Falls was the choice of Vulcan Rex.

Yet another Carnival group was that of the Hussars who greeted visiting dignitaries during the Carnivals of 1916 and 1917 and guarded Boreas and the Queen of the Snows in these Carnivals. Marching clubs in these two Carnivals were asked to identify their tallest men for Hussar-duty. The idea was revived in 1937. That year the twenty-five Hussars, all at least six-feet tall, wore black and red uniforms with red leather boots and black lambskin shakos as headgear (*St. Paul Dispatch*, January 12, 1937, 1A). Forrest Wold was one of those involved in reviving the Carnival and, according to a later account, was largely responsible for the formation of the King's Guard (*St. Paul Pioneer Press*, January 28, 1968, *Pictorial Magazine*, 20). For later Carnivals members of the Hussars were recruited from R.O.T.C. units at local colleges, including Hamline, Macalester and St. Thomas. In 1959 the St. Paul Jaycees began to help the Carnival and the guards' organization recruit guards. Today those who wish to join the six-to-twelve member unit of Royal Guards (as they are now called) apply as do other Winter Carnival participants. Guard officers include a captain, sergeant, and commander. In Winter Carnival parades the Royal Guards ride on a 1952 Army-style vehicle known as the Trooper, which is painted blue. Floats are the platforms for Klondike Kate, junior and senior royalty, and the Royal Family.

Most of the Hussars or Guards, Wind Princes, Wind Princesses, the Prime Ministers and

Vulcanus' Krewe were added as legend characters by 1940. In the 1940s a Klondike Kate singer had entertained at the Gay Nineties Gold Rush Drink Emporium and Dance Hall at the Hotel St. Paul. In 1971 the St. Paul Jaycees decided to raise funds via a casino with entertainment provided by that buxom beauty of the Yukon. The casino was a success and Klondike Kate became an annual featured attraction, selected after a talent competition. The competition and the character are now handled by the Order of Klondike Kates. A recent version of the Carnival legend suggests that Vulcanus has fallen in love with Klondike Kate and spends Carnival season chasing her in addition to his other activities. Klondike Kate sometimes runs with the Vulcans, but may join the Royal Family at other events. She is the only legend character to "go both ways" in her loyalties.

The Klondike Kate show in the Hotel St. Paul was a Carnival fixture during the 1940s. Courtesy of Helen Duffy Murphy.

Klondike Kate entertained at the Gay Nineties Bar in the Hotel St. Paul during the Victory Carnival of 1946. Oversize postcard invitation courtesy of Eugene DiMartino.

KLONDIKE KATES

1971	CAROL CARNEY
1972	SHIRLEY GUSTAFSON
1973	SHIRLEY LITE JONES
1974	DOROTHY FREYBERGER
1975	SHARI KAYE STELTZER
1976	BILLIE JEAN MORSETH
1977	SANDY WYLIE
1978	CLAUDETTE RIESCHL
1979	DIANA WEBBER
1980	TRISH STEFFENSON
1981	PAT VIDEEN
1982	SCOTTIE MCFARLAND
1983	PATTI LEIVERMAN
1984	JEANNE CUMMINGS
1985	CONSTANCE CROWELL
1986	DIANNE PINE
1987	NANCY BAUER MOSHER
1988	NANCY FISCHBACH
1989	CINDY CHEYNE
1990	CELESTE GAGLIARDI
1991	PATTY PALODICHUCK
1992	LIZ MANBECK
1993	LOIS LAURIE
1994	LINDA UNDERHILL
1995	BARBARA SORENSON
1996	PHYLLIS CHICKETT
1997	SHAR SALISBURY
1998	RENEE JACKSON
1999	BARB YOZAMP
2000	JUDY SELL NELSON
2001	WENDY MAUSOLF
2002	DOLLY SPARBER
2003	KIM TSOUKALAS

*Klondike Kates appear at the
1990 Vulcan Conclave at the
Town and Country Club.*

*Dianne Pine, the Klondike
Kate for 1986, checks her
music.*

The Winter Carnival has two other royal courts. King Winter and his Queen of the Northlands represent the city's senior citizens. Candidates are nominated by senior organizations and selected by a committee. The senior royals have been chosen annually since 1958. Their counterparts, King Frost and his Queen of the Snowflakes, are part of a junior court of twelve members. Recreation centers throughout the city name candidates for these crowns in a tradition which dates back to 1949.

For all members of the Winter Carnival cast the festival days are crowded. There are floats to ride in the day and night parades, attendance at the Coronation Ball, the Storming of Boreas' palace, and the events scheduled by their particular group (Queens, Vulcans, Winds, Guards, and Fire and Brimstone). Once the Carnival is finished both Boreas and his Court and the Vulcans begin their schedule of festival and community appearances, together or separately, depending on the invitation. The Aberdeen (South Dakota), Snow Fest; Gasparilla Days in Tampa, Florida; the Minneapolis Aquatennial; the Festival du Voyageur in Winnipeg, Canada; and the Seattle Seafair have been regular destinations. When St. Paul was named an All-American City in 1955 a link with the Tournament of Roses began. Until 1969 the Theo. Hamm Brewing Company sponsored a St. Paul Winter Carnival float ridden by each year's Boreas, Queen of the Snows, and Prime Minister, in the Rose parade. In his usual happy fashion the Hamm's Bear, made of dark brown flowers, tried to show Californians how Minnesotans celebrated winter. Riding on the floral-covered Tournament of Roses float was a many hours-long experience, as Gary Hiebert noted in his Preface. Muriel Lux Schlitgen, Queen of the Snows in 1960, recalled one particular refrain from her ride. The float driver could only see the road through a small window. Fred Soderberg, that year's Boreas Rex, stood near the window and, every so often, his long Borgana (artificial fur) cape would drape itself over the driver's window. Quickly, from below, a voice would then call out, "Move your cape, Boris!"

Joining with the Minneapolis Aquatennial and the Minnesota Department of Tourism, the St. Paul Winter Carnival continued to sponsor a Rose parade float until 1978. Dan Dolan (Boreas Rex XLII) and Marlene Richter (Queen of the Snows) were the last to ride the Minnesota float. Mary Lou Lipke, Queen of the Snows in 1954, was said to be the most traveled queen, since her appearances ranged from Alaska to Florida, and from Portland and Seattle to New Orleans (*St. Paul Pioneer Press*, Roto Magazine, January 30, 1955).

The 1947 Dinner of the Kings was the opportunity to salute the newly chosen Boreas Rex (Robert Albrecht) as well as his predecessors.

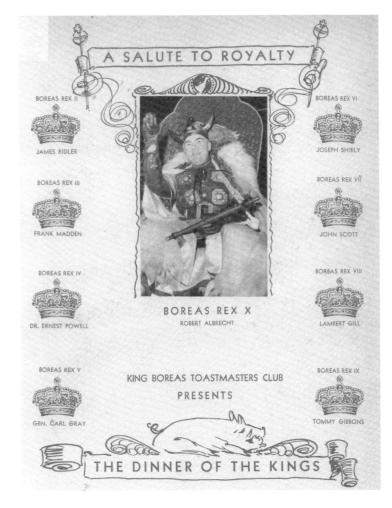

A SALUTE TO ROYALTY

BOREAS REX II — JAMES RIDLER
BOREAS REX III — FRANK MADDEN
BOREAS REX IV — DR. ERNEST POWELL
BOREAS REX V — GEN. CARL GRAY

BOREAS REX X
ROBERT ALBRECHT

BOREAS REX VI — JOSEPH SHIELY
BOREAS REX VII — JOHN SCOTT
BOREAS REX VIII — LAMBERT GILL
BOREAS REX IX — TOMMY GIBBONS

KING BOREAS TOASTMASTERS CLUB
PRESENTS

THE DINNER OF THE KINGS

Tournament
of Roses

ST. PAUL WINTER CARNIVAL

HIAWATHA'S TRAVELS FROM THE LAND OF SKY BLUE WATERS

*The 1967 Winter
Carnival Float in the
Pasadena Tournament
of Roses parade. Winter
Carnival royalty sit
under Hiawatha's feather
headdress. Courtesy
of the author.*

PRIME MINISTERS

1896	SAMUEL VAN SANT, Lord High Chancellor
1939	JOSEPH J. MITCHELL
1940	JOSEPH J. MITCHELL
1941	PATRICK J. TOWLE
1942	ROBERT V. RENSCH
1946	ROBERT L. UTNE
1947	M. WALTER SIME
1948	ALLEN R. LINDGREN
1949	HUBERT W. WHITE, JR.
1950	HENRI G. FOUSSARD
1951	JAY P. O'CONNOR
1952	WESLEY M. CHANDLER
1953	ORION WINFORD
1954	PETER R. HINSCH
1955	ARNOLD H. BOCKSTRUCK

1956	J. PETER DEVINE
1957	ROGER FOUSSARD
1958	JOHN H. BURG
1959	R. PATRICK EGAN
1960	CARL W. CUMMINS, JR.
1961	RICHARD T. MURPHY
1962	GARETH HIEBERT
1963	LAWRENCE J. HAYES
1964	WILLIAM J. HUOT
1965	JOHN H. KISSINGER
1966	DANIEL F. DOLAN
1967	BOB CARTER, SR.
1968	DON VALENTO
1969	RICHARD G. PALEN
1970	GIL THOELE, JR.
1971	MARVIN ELLISON
1972	DONN J. EIDEN
1973	BERT J. MCKASY
1974	JAY A. PFAENDER
1975	ROGER THOMPSON
1976	ROBERT SHEILD
1977	RICHARD BARBARI
1978	ANDREW FREEMAN
1979	MICHAEL LETHERT
1980	DAN OLSON
1981	DAVID W. LARSON
1982	PHIL JUNGWIRTH
1983	BILL LALONDE
1984	GORDON SCHMUCK
1985	GORDON GUTZMANN
1986	DAVID MCDONELL
1987	TIM HUGHES
1988	MARK SWANSON
1989	TED ZWIEG
1990	MONTE JOHNSON
1991	TERRY DAVERN
1992	DAVE JOHNSON
1993	MATT MCDONOUGH
1994	JOHANNA MOHWINKEL
1995	DICK BEROVER
1996	DENNIS BOOM
1997	ANN MARIE REIM
1998	JODY LINGOFELT
1999	STEVE LEAFEREN
1900	DAVE MCDONALD
2001	STEVE SNELLING
2002	DICK KEHR
2003	GREGORY M. SHEEHAN

Boreases and Queens of the Snows have attended World's Fairs in Seattle and in Brussels, Belgium. They have christened trains, ships and airplanes, and welcomed the stars of movies, television and radio to St. Paul. In Minnesota and surrounding states they appear in many town festivals. One of the first trips made by Carnival royalty was probably that of Carnival clubs, Gloriana, and the Lord High Chamberlain to New Ulm in 1896. That city was celebrating its own winter festival complete with sports, parades, and an ice palace. Julius Berndt, architect of that New Ulm ice palace, is best known for the temple high on a New Ulm hill, on which the statue of Herman the German stands. Although the weather was miserable the St. Paul clubs marched in a short parade to the Union house where, it was reported, "everything was free" and Gloriana rode her horse into the saloon (*St. Paul Globe*, February 9, 1896).

In the Twin Cities Carnival royalty visit schools, hospitals, orphanages, and neighborhood parades, often numbering several hundred events. Carnival royalty speak of making "appearances," but Vulcans talk instead of the "runs" they make, as firefighters do. Although it is understood that the Winter Carnival family is representing the city of St. Paul, travel costs are either paid by the Royal Family or their respective sponsors.

At the conclusion of the Winter Carnival year, Boreas, the Queen of the Snows, Guards, Winds, Princesses and Vulcanus and his Krewe are all invited to join alumni organizations. The Star of Boreas, the Former Queens club, the Order of Royal Guards, the Imperial Order of Fire and Brimstone, the Council of Fire Kings, the Order of the Klondike Kates, and the Churchill Club (for former Prime Ministers) all welcome the outgoing legend characters as members. (The original Queens Club, founded in 1958, was limited to the ladies of 1916-1917.) Each of these clubs meets regularly throughout the year, sponsors various events during Carnival week, and takes part in the work of the Carnival, often choosing and mentoring their successors. Each club sends a representative to the Uniformed Groups Council, founded in 1976, which speaks for them in Carnival affairs. The Queens Tea, held at the home of Helen Duffy Murphy (Queen of the Snows in 1947) since 1968, is not only a chance for the former queens to gather, but an opportunity for them to meet the upcoming Carnival's queen candidates and query them. Candidates are asked to answer questions devised by the former queens. The judges' committee listens to their responses and considers their poise and composure. The Vulcan Victory Dance, held on the last weekend of Carnival, is a similar event, introducing the new Krewe and Vulcanus Rex, newly unveiled, to Fire and Brimstone members.

The logo of the Imperial Order of Fire and Brimstone, the organization for the Vulcans and their Krewes. Courtesy of John Meyers.

Vulcans on a "run" in one of their fire trucks. Courtesy of John Meyers.

As Robert Lavenda pointed out in his study of Minnesota festivals, *Corn Fests and Winter Carnivals* (1997), the Carnival participants have usually been chosen from certain age groups. Boreas Rex and Vulcanus Rex are usually older than the Wind Princes, the Prime Minister, the Vulcan Krewe and the Royal Guards, in that order. Financial obligations are also greater for the two kings than for the other Carnival participants since the kings pay for the traditional meals, buttons, and their uniforms, as well as for travel.

A chart based on Lavenda's research indicates the age bracket of the costumed characters, their financial obligations, and how they are selected:

Number	Character	Sex, Age	Cost to Serve	How Selected
1	Boreas Rex	Male, late 40s, early 50s	$40,000	invitation
1	Queen of the Snows	Female, 20-35 years	$1,500	competition
1	Vulcanus Rex	Male, late 40, early 50s	$15,000	invitation
1	Prime Minister	Male or female, 30 to 40	$10,000	invitation
4	Princes of the Winds	Male, early 40s	$10,000	application
7	Vulcan Krewe	Male, over 25	$4,000	application
10	Royal Guards	Male, 25 to 30	$1,500	application
4	Wind Princesses	Female, 20 to 35	$1,500	application
1	Klondike Kate	Female, over 21	not available	competition

Men desiring to join the Vulcan Krewe apply to the Imperial Order of Fire and Brimstone. If selected, they agree to keep that information secret until the unmasking at Carnival's end. The seven Krewe members pledge to participate for five years in Krewe activities. After the first year these Krewe members mentor the new Krewe, in the third year they sell Vulcan charms, in the fourth year they conduct a fund-raiser for the organization, and in the fifth year they organize the Vulcan Victory Dance.

In the early 1990s a committee reexamined the Carnival legend and roles and recommended administrative changes. Now queen candidates must be over 18 and high school graduates, but there is no upper age limit or marital status restriction as there once was (two previous Queens of the Snow resigned during their reigns when they married). Maureen Damman (Queen of the Snows in 1996) was the first married woman selected for the role since Mrs. L. L. Cook in 1886, although, it should be noted, 1941's Queen married during her reign and kept her crown. Three women have served as Prime Minister to date: Johanna Mohwinkel in 1994, Ann Marie Reim in 1997, and Jody Lingofelt in 1998. Women have joined the Royal Guards and, as it will be recalled, the Daisy Queen of 1896 was a man.

Several columnists in the *St. Paul Pioneer Press* attacked the basis of selecting the Queen of the Snows, charging that "legends change." Amy Gage argued that "the issue boiled down to nothing less than the role of women in society, whether they're valued more for youth or experience, and who among them deserves to represent the city of St. Paul" (*St. Paul Pioneer Press*, January 19, 1997). Boreas Rex had traditionally been selected on the basis of his achievements and, as a business executive, his ability to contribute time and money to the task. Queen Aurora, once nominated or elected to represent the business where she worked, was selected for beauty rather than achievement and critics felt that should change. The former Queens believed the criticism made them all sound like "cookie cutter" duplicates. So, said Helen Duffy Murphy proudly, the former Queens changed and for the first time took on a fundraising and philanthropic mission. They now organize a yearly luncheon whose proceeds are donated to the Children's Home Society.

Dressing The Part

Vital to the Winter Carnival are its moments of pageantry: parades, coronations, and the storming of the royal palace. The characters in the Carnival legend each have a role to play and need suitable costumes. But what should those costumes be?

Thirty major roles function in Carnival pageantry each year. Twenty-four are usually played by men, depending on how many Royal Guards are enlisted. Women's roles are far fewer. They include the Queen of the Snows, her four Wind Princesses, and Klondike Kate. The queen and the princesses wear basic formal attire: a white ball gown and a cape for the queen, and simpler matching formal gowns for the princesses. According to Dot Bentfield, the Royal Seamstress, the colors for the princesses' gowns are red for South, blue for North, green or brown for West, and purple for East. For their other appearances they don clothing appropriate to the occasion: dresses, suits, slacks, winter sportswear and, always, white gloves. Klondike Kates dress as saloon singers of the 1890s in Alaska. They favor red, black, satins and laces.

Deciding how Boreas should look has been a puzzle. The nineteenth century Ice King was seen as a late winter Santa Claus by cartoonists, although Borealis Rex I (in 1886) attended his coronation and parade outfitted as the Sun King, Louis XIV of France. Newspaper sketches show him wearing a coat, vest, short satin pants and hose. The second Borealis chose to appear as a Viking with fur robes, while Borealis Rex III and IV wore the floor length garments suitable for a medieval king or a Kris Kringle.

For the 1916 and 1917 Outdoor Sports

Each Ice King chooses his own uniform, as did Lambert Gill (Boreas Rex VIII) in 1942.

C. H. Bevington and Edna Bolke were crowned King and Queen of the 1928 Midway Carnival at the Hippodrome. Courtesy of Midway Chamber of Commerce.

Carnivals Boreas wore a short tunic, tights, and a fur cape. Distinctive circles on his royal tunic in 1917 suggest the outfit of Kings or Jacks from a deck of cards. Martin Giesen, whose family firm supplied theatrical and masquerade costumes for many years in St. Paul, probably made the costumes for the Carnival pageant since Louis W. Hill requested sketches from him. Boreas' costume was made by Finch, Van Slyke, and McConville.

In Carnival photographs from both years marching club queens appear indoors or outside in either a version of their club uniform or in a fur trimmed coat and hat, often with a muff. In a letter dated November 24, 1916, Carnival secretary C. R. Vincent asked the marching clubs to limit the expenditures for queens' costumes to less than $100 so there would not be an unnecessary rivalry between the clubs.

The three queens who presided over the Midway Outdoor Sports Carnivals were selected from the district's playgrounds and, perhaps for that reason, appeared in sports attire. Edna Bolke, the 1928 queen, wore a leather jacket, jodhpurs, and boots at her coronation. A drawing of Ms. Bolke appeared on buttons and posters for that year's Carnival. Helen Webb, Queen Midway in 1929, presided over an Indian theme event so her coronation dress included bead necklaces and a feather in her hair.

Reviving the Carnival in 1937 meant rewriting its legend and rethinking costumes for the characters. No longer was a playing card Jack the model. Instead, cues were taken from uniforms of European royalty, George VI of England and Carol of Romania. Mrs. John F. Scott, wife of Boreas VII (1941), planned a uniform for her hus-

Three Boreases, all in their Ice King uniforms, in 1953. Courtesy of the Midway Chamber of Commerce.

band in navy blue like the admiral's uniform worn by the English king. Gold cord, epaulets and tassels decorated the jacket. His doeskin cape was patterned after one worn by the Romanian king, but with crossed skis emblazoned on it. When not wearing the Carnival crown he donned a curved admiral's hat, such as Napoleon wore, but with an explosion of gold braid covering it.

Most of the later Ice Kings and their Prime Ministers would choose a version of a military uniform with a fur or fabric lined cape for Carnival wear. Boreas is expected to wear blue, but that isn't a rigid protocol. Ice Kings have appeared in white, blue, green or Vulcan red, at their option. For many years Daniel Nordgren at the Maurice L. Rothschild's men's clothing store was the Royal Tailor. Nordgren kept photographs of military and royal uniforms for his Carnival clients. He could even supply imitation medals should a Boreas desire an array to jingle on his jacket.

One of the post-World War II Ice Kings decided on a different theme for his costume. He, and his Prime Minister, would be Vikings. After checking the details with an authority on the Vikings at the University of Minnesota, Robert Albrecht (Boreas Rex X) had the costumes made. Both men wore leather jerkins with belts and cloth skirts underneath. Both wore fur leggings with criss-cross leather bands around, leather shoes, breastplates and helmets. Part of Boreas' costume was a polar bear skin cape with the head fitted like a parka over his helmet. The Viking costumes, and a fur cloak worn by the year's Queen of the Snows, Helen Duffy, were made by that Ice King's family business, Albrecht Furs.

As the man who will serve as Boreas has usually been selected by late summer he has plenty of time to order the necessary uniforms. The Wind

Princes also have months in which to assemble their costumes. But for the Queen of the Snows and her four Wind Princesses the situation is quite different. They are not selected until Coronation day and they will need some regal attire immediately. The solution over the years has been to assemble appropriate clothing ahead of time and then alter the garments which don't quite fit the new Queen and Princesses.

Various St. Paul stores have provided the Queen's all-white wardrobe over the years. Buyers from Field-Schlick, Frank Murphy, and the Mutchlers of David-Edwins women's store all supplied the clothing from the 1950s on. In one newspaper interview article Jake Mutchler recalled that designers across the country knew well that the Carnival needed a wardrobe in white. More recently the Saint Paul Festival and Heritage Foundation has allocated a budget of $1,200 for the Queen's clothing and $600 for each Wind Princess. A committee from the Ambassadors (once known as the Women's Division) shops for appropriate clothing in approximate sizes. As soon as the Queen and princesses are crowned the seamstresses go to work. Dot Bentfield says that she and her crew arrive at the headquarters hotel with the clothing and their sewing machines the evening before. As soon as the Coronation Ball is over the now royal ladies try on dresses and see what needs to be altered. One former queen stores ball gowns from previous years which could possibly be worn again.

For all of the Carnival royalty some items are theirs to keep while others will be handed on to the next queen, prince, or king. Each Boreas receives a scepter and crown and his queen is given a tiara. Their mantles (or long cloaks) are worn only at the Queen's coronation. According

Boreas Rex X (Robert Albrecht) and his Queen of the Snows (Helen Duffy) ride in a Midway parade, 1947. Courtesy of Helen Duffy Murphy.

Boreas Rex XI (Edward C. Hampe) presides over a Midway meeting, 1948. Courtesy of the Midway Chamber of Commerce.

The Royal Family of
Boreas Rex XLIV
(Norman Mears) in
1980. The King, Queen
and Prime Minister are
in the center, the four
Wind Princesses stand
next to the Wind Princes,
with Royal Guards posed
in the back row.

The Royal Family of
Boreas Rex LVIII (Ted
Zwieg) in 1994. Included
is the first woman Prime
Minister and a woman
who was a Royal Guard.

to Lorraine Venaas, who served on the Coronation Committee for many years, the original mantles were purchased in New Orleans in 1938 and had actual fur borders. When these royal garments became too worn to wear, new ones were made locally. Gold lamé panels are in the center, decorated with hundreds of sequins sewn in a snowflake design on Boreas' mantle, and in a flower design for the Queen's cloak. When the mantles are placed on their shoulders, the eighteen-foot length and great weight makes support by the pages necessary. The East Wind prince's name is engraved on a sword that will be used by his successors.

Fire Kings wear black suits and capes or at least since the 1980s they have. According to Steve Popovich, Vulcanus Rex XLVIII, dressing the Fire King in black keeps him from being confused with his Krewe, who are clad in identical red outfits. Ignis Rex (in 1916) wore a coat, a long braided belt, and a close fitting cap with horns. Both he and his 1917 successor could be easily identified as they were mask-less. The 1917 Fire King's garb was in the same deck-of-cards style as that of the Ice King. Change came with Ernie Reiff, Vulcan Rex VI in 1940. Reiff and his wife devised the red snowmobile (or "running") suits for the Krewe with the red fitted caps. Vulcan Rex and his Krewe have worn black horns or feathers on their red caps, and once wore uncomfortable black masks over their eyes. Their "rooster" caps have a ridge down the center and they have worn black goggles since 1974. Most decorate their faces with beards and mustaches, using black greasepaint, a tube of which they carry in a shoulder pocket.

The Fire King can carry a sword, and it once damaged Vulcan himself. Adolph Bremer, the 1941 Fire King, slipped and fell, breaking three of his ribs and bending the tip of the sword (*St. Paul Pioneer Press*, February 1, 1953). Vulcans in the past were famous for the cheek-to-cheek "smudge" or kiss that they gave on occasion to unwilling targets, but the smudge was abandoned after protests in the 1970s. Now a Vulcan marks a grease paint "V" if the recipient is willing. The "V" is supposed to indicate that the person so marked is a friend to Vulcan rather than part of the camp of Boreas.

On the tunic of Vulcan suits is an embroidered torch with the name of the Krewe member (such as Prince of Ashes or Count Embrious) above it. General Flameous, traditionally the member of the Vulcan Krewe with military experience, once carried a gun that was fired during parades or as a signal when the Krewe was about to leave a tavern, but he no longer does that. The cowboy-dressed West Wind Prince is allowed to shoot his gun during parade appearances. Each year, at the end of the reign of Vulcanus Rex and his Krewe, the heavy cape and the running suits are returned to the Imperial Order of Fire and Brimstone. The two Kings, of Fire and Ice, both wear formal jackets in ceremonial appearances. Boreas Rex wears an Eisenhower-style Army tuxedo jacket with a cummerbund. The red jacket of the Fire Kings is known as the "flame coat" because of the gold flames outlined in red on the front and sleeves. Local columnist Joe Soucheray once commented that the flame coats made them look like "walking 1957 Chevrolet hot rods. They

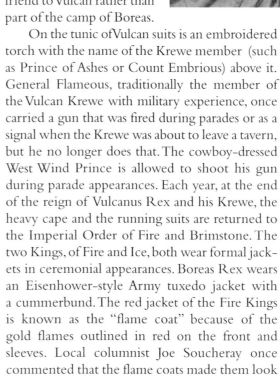

A Vulcan is permitted to "smooch" a willing victim. Vulcan Rex XV (Larry Hodgson) and Mary Linehan (the Fire Prevention Queen) demonstrate in 1952. Courtesy of Denny and Mary Harris.

looked beautiful" (*St. Paul Pioneer Press*, January 30, 1991, 7A). Vulcanus Rex and his Krewe celebrate the unexpected and the fun of Carnival. They have rules, however, which must be respected so when a new group of red jacketed merrymakers appeared, the men of Fire and Brimstone were not pleased. In 1991 Leo Gadbois, owner of two taverns near Selby and Dale avenues, sponsored the Vulcanettes. In this new fiery group, waitresses from his establishments wore red silk capes, jackets, ties and cummerbunds and eye masks. The sign of the Vulcanettes was marked in red grease paint, usually smudged, on the faces of men. After the Fire and Brimstone organization threatened legal action, the dispute between Vulcans and Vulcanettes was settled out of court. The Vulcanettes agreed not to make any appearances at official Winter Carnival events, although they could appear elsewhere.

A dinner reunion of former Fire Kings at the North Oaks Golf Club, 1971.

A sticker from Vulcanus Rex XXXIV (Bob Flakne), 1971. Courtesy of John Meyers.

Vulcanettes had their headquarters at Sweeney's bar. Courtesy of the author.

Wrapped In Plaid

When planning was begun for the first Winter Carnival, in the fall of 1885, it was clear that parade participants would need uniforms. While the legend characters could tap the resources of St. Paul theatrical costume makers, such as Giesen's, for individual outfits, uniforms for the marching clubs, dozens strong, needed an industrial firm to do the work. Style, too, was a concern. What should members of these new toboggan clubs wear as they marched in sub-zero weather?

Like the plans for the Ice Palace itself, the earliest uniform designs came from Montreal via the St. George's Snow-Shoe Club. Blankets were the basic material supplemented by flannel, embroidery, and fur, if desired. Wrote one reporter:

The costume for gentlemen consists of two garments, a loose fitting blouse reaching to within a few inches of the knees, and provided with a belt and capote [hood] and knee breeches... Long, heavy woolen stockings to correspond in color with the uniform, a heavy woolen sash, knitted toque, or cap, and a pair of moccasins complete the outfit for men. Nearly every club has a membership of ladies, and they make the best of comrades. They are plucky and active, and endure fatigue better than many of their male companions. Their suits are made of the same material as are the men's. They consist of a loose waist with a broad belt, and a skirt reaching to about the tops of ordinary boots. They wear leggings and moccasins, a waist sash, and jaunty caps, sometimes a flat, Scotch style, and sometimes toques (Brick Pomeroy's Democrat, *December 15, 1886*).

According to the *St. Paul Pioneer Press* (January 15, 1886) the entire man's outfit could be purchased for $13.50 or one could buy blankets wholesale for $3.50 each and create three suits from one blanket.

Blanket material covered the marchers once more in Louis Hill's Outdoor Sports Carnivals of 1916 and 1917. Most marching clubs were no longer the Indian-named affinity groups of friends of the 1880s who wanted to tramp, snowshoe, or toboggan together. The marching clubs of 1916 and 1917 were usually sponsored by local businesses. Rather than the social Nushka Club of the 1880s, parade-watchers saw ranks of identically clad employees of Griggs-Cooper or the green-striped marchers of the Minnehaha Dry Cleaning Company marching club. Each club elected a queen who either wore the club uniform or a fur trimmed coat and hat. The uniform style for men was now a jacket, often

double breasted, with a wide belt, breeches, boots and heavy wool stockings, and a winter cap. Women in most groups wore long coats or jackets with skirts whose hems reached down to the tops of their boots. Woolen mills had been contacted by the Carnival committees so that adequate blanketing fabric was available for purchase. In a letter to the Pendleton Woolen Mills, Louis W. Hill placed an order for 3,000 yards of the 26 ounce Yellowstone blankets with red and yellow stripes, and similar amounts of white with red and blue stripes, yellow and blue stripes, and yellow or orange with black stripes. In addition, the Carnival wanted Hudson Bay blankets, in magenta, red, royal purple, and blue (Letter of Louis W. Hill, Sr., to Roy T. Bishop, October 14, 1916. Hill Papers).

An interesting commentary on the blanket uniforms was written by C. M. Flandrau, son of Borealis Rex IV and, like his father, a celebrated and witty author. During the Carnival period many wore their costumes daily. Flandrau thought they were:

warm, beautiful, becoming clothes that are significant of our locality and adapted to our strenuous climate... Somehow or other, dramatically speaking, these gay blanket-made clothes struck throughout a very remarkable "right note." In every possible fashion, practical or pictorial, they seemed to belong to us as a community; they "went" with our brilliant sunshine, our mountains of snow and our terrible temperature... (St. Paul Pioneer Press, *February 6, 1916*).

Turning the blankets into uniforms was done by St. Paul businesses, one of whom advertised that he could make 25 or 100 uniforms in the weeks before the Carnival (*St. Paul Daily News*, January 7, 1917, 5). The resulting clothing

Frank H. Davis poses in a homemade 1886 Carnival marching suit.

1916 Badges from Carnival Marching Clubs. The polar bear behind the "N" is a Nushka patch, H/S is for the High School, and N & C is for Noyes Brothers, and Cutler. Courtesy of the J. J. Hill Library.

was solid color, plaid or white with the three or four broad stripes familiar from Hudson's Bay blankets. The three or four point Hudson's Bay fabric was worn by the Glacier Park marching club, the largest parade group, as well as by Louis Hill himself. One of Hill's frock coats had additional beadwork on the back as well as a capote (hood). For the evening or torchlight parade every marcher was expected to carry a torch, flambeau, or other lighting device.

By far the largest group to participate in the Carnivals of 1916 and 1917 included employees from Louis Hill's Northern Pacific Railroad. There were marching clubs, a hockey team, fourteen trumpeters, three blanket-bouncing squads, a drill team, and a glee club. A small booklet shows all of the members of the different groups. Photographed by the official Winter Carnival photographer, Camera Art, the cover resembles in both colors and style the official souvenir book. Louise Schilling, Northern Pacific's Carnival queen, is shown in a Carnival Girl pose in her red coat against the Railroad's yin/yang symbol.

One group which marched together in the 1916 and 1917 Carnivals in unmatched uniforms (although wearing similar tall hats) was that of the Hussars. Carnival organizers had asked each marching club to select their tallest man for service as guards, so the Hussar group photograph shows uniforms in a dizzying mix of stripes and plaids. When the Royal Guards were formed in 1937 men at least six feet tall were sought as members. Hussars greeted any visiting dignitaries at the train station. They were alerted fifteen minutes ahead of train arrivals by the boom of a cannon fired from the roof of the Pioneer building.

Women had been discouraged from marching in some of the 1880s parades, but that was not the case thirty years later. Women worked in many of the businesses sponsoring marching units. There were even all-women marching groups such as the contingent from the Women's Civic League (they each carried an elegant muff) and the students from Miss Loomis' school for girls.

In 1937 one woman even suggested that there be a housewives marching club so that those who otherwise stayed home could be included in the fun of the Carnival.

By 1937 blanket uniforms and the warm wool toboggan suits of the nineteenth century parades were no longer available. While some remained in private hands or were donated to museums, many of the earlier uniforms were

Irene Corwin Snyder and Neil Snyder pose in their 1916 marching club uniforms. She belonged to the Weequah Canoe Club; he marched with the Northwestern Electric Equipment Company. Courtesy of Marge Montillon.

*The 1916 checkerboard uni-
forms, toy dogs, and float of
Wilcox Trux were distinctive.*

*1917 Souvenir program of
the Northern Pacific Railroad
Carnival Marching Club.
Courtesy of Walt and
Lynn Hedblum.*

SAINT PAUL
CARNIVAL
.. 9 1 7 ..
HELP TO MAKE
IT A HOTTER ONE
MEET ME AT THE
N.P. CLUB ROOMS

YELLOWSTONE PARK LINE
AND ROUTE OF THE GREAT
BIG BAKED POTATO ·
· ·
NORTHERN PACIFIC BOOSTERS
SCATTERED AROUND THE
WORLD FORM AN EMPIRE
ON WHICH THE SUN NEVER
SETS

sent to Finland as part of a World War I relief effort in 1918 (*St. Paul Pioneer Press*, January 26, 1990, C2). One exception was the uniform of the Minnehaha Dry Cleaners Club. Sufficient uniforms had evidently been saved so the club wore their green and white striped garments in the 1937 parade. The next style for uniforms was the shiny fabric jacket and pants commonly worn by the marching bands. Women could wear either pants or skirts with their jackets. While marching clubs had usually trained together before the Carnival parades, well-rehearsed drill teams with drum majors and majorettes increasingly became part of Carnivals beginning in the 1940s.

Important to all the marching groups were their uniforms, shoulder patches or other insignia, and items which they carried such as cow bells or canes.

Businesses that made outdoor clothing or sold furs certainly took the opportunity to exhibit their wares, but usually that sort of product display was found in the Industrial Parades. Two companies, however, displayed products in parade uniforms and their creativity was fondly remembered. In the 1928 Midway Outdoor Sports Carnival parade the Waldorf Paper Company (now, Rock-Tenn Corporation) had marchers and float riders dressed in corrugated boxes from square heads to equally rigid legs. The paper boxes were a big hit, but proved far from easy to wear. If a paper box-clad marcher were to fall, like Humpty Dumpty, help was needed to help him rise. Paper box paraders only appeared once, but the Hilex gnomes, shaped like large drops of bleach, were part of Carnival parades for decades.

The paper box marchers of the Waldorf Paper Products Company march in the evening parade of the 1928 Carnival. Courtesy of the Midway Chamber of Commerce.

Grande, Torchlight, and Industrial Parades

4

Of all the components of the Winter Carnival, from sports to races, and ice palaces to parades, it was the parades which were probably the easiest element for the first committees to organize. Parades had been done before in Minnesota, in fact as recently as 1883.

Probably the city's first significant march around the downtown area of St. Paul took place in September of 1858. The Atlantic Cable had been completed, making faster telegraphic communication possible between England and the United States. St. Paul and many other American cities heralded this achievement with a parade involving local political and military leaders on horseback or in carriages. The Pioneer Guards, the state's oldest military regiment, marched, followed by the city's fire department. What struck observers most was the Pioneer Printing Company's wagon pulled by six horses. It carried an exhibit about printing, and about the life of Benjamin Franklin. Next came Miss Azelene Allen, an actress then appearing in St. Paul, who rode a wagon devoted to the arts. She held a spear with a cap of liberty on it, representing the Goddess of Liberty. Frank Moore, who wrote about the Atlantic cable com-

memoration, noted that the St. Paul city council appropriated "several hundred dollars" to help pay for the parade and illumination.

The next major parade also celebrated completion, but this time of the railroad. In 1883 it was time to celebrate the completion of Henry Villard's Northern Pacific railroad from the Mississippi river to the West coast. Villard had invited American political leaders (President Chester A. Arthur and Ulysses S. Grant), European financiers, journalists and photographers to join in the celebration. The Hotel Lafayette on Lake Minnetonka was the rendezvous for Villard's guests. They dined, spent the night, and then witnessed giant, separate parades. Minneapolis' was fifteen miles long, and St. Paul's five miles longer! Each involved hundreds of horse-drawn wagons and carriages whose route was decorated with flags, bunting, pine boughs, and six temporary street-corner arches celebrating Villard's triumph. After the parades the 200 visitors left by excursion train for their hotel, and then for the golden spike ceremony on September 8, 1883, in Montana territory.

Parades have usually been organized in divisions. For the Villard guests the sixth or industrial division was the largest of all in the parade, needing more than two and one half hours to pass in review. Wagons were decorated with slogans and evergreen branches. Although the parade was described as "not a conspicuous attempt at advertising," what every business did was clear from the displays of products, employees at work, or even samples distributed to the crowds. The parade demonstrated how everybody would benefit from the completion of the railroad, and stressed its importance to the city. Aboard the *Pioneer Press* wagon workers printed

Trade card published in 1888 by the St. Paul branch of the Goodyear Rubber Company. Courtesy of Walt and Lynn Hedblum.

COMPLIMENTS OF
GOODYEAR RUBBER CO.

copies of the Sunday edition on a steam-powered press, distributing thousands of newspapers as it drove along.

Many firms simply piled their wagons high with examples of the clothing, canned foods, or fur robes they sold. Employees of Adam Fetsch, a cigar maker, were seated on his wagon, making cigars as they rode and handing them out to the eager crowds. On other wagons men worked on trunks, harnesses and barrels. The 1,500 wagons of the Villard parade set a standard for an industrial parade that later Winter Carnival committees would seek to equal.

One newspaper writer commented:

*In conclusion, St. Paul may never look on the like again, for it seems hardly probable that so vast an opportunity for self-congratulation can ever be presented by the future. The people of the city looked upon the time as the turn in affairs which guarantees development into a mighty metropolis; perhaps the last occasion when 100,000 people can be made to feel the greatest personal interest in a demonstration of joyfulness (*St. Paul Pioneer Press, September 4, 1883).*

Just over two years later, in January of 1886, the next parade committee would watch the results of their efforts. The 1883 parade may have been longer, but for the first Winter Carnival there were more times for self-congratulation as they staged a daytime "Grande" parade, an evening Torchlight parade, a short masquerade procession, and yet another event organized by the German-American community.

The Atlantic Cable parade had involved units on foot, on horseback, and riding in carriages. With the 1883 parade the emphasis was placed on horse-drawn wagons. Both of these parades were held in the early fall so any problems posed by snowy, slippery streets would not concern parade planners. But a series of January marches would be quite different.

Parade planners selected their routes and encouraged businesses along those streets to decorate their premises. In 1858 flags, bunting, evergreen boughs and all manner of illumination could be seen along the streets. For the 1883 Villard parade and for the 1893 Great Northern celebration giant, detailed papier-mâché arches marked street intersections. Stereopticon images present the arches which showed trains and carried text emphasizing the railroad's link with the West.

Arches in 1886 crossed the streets, resting on four columns, one on each corner. The framework was of wood, covered with evergreens. Along the face of each span was a perforated pipe of gas jets covered with small colored globes. At night, reported the *St. Paul Daily Globe,* "the sight is one that can scarcely be surpassed in its brilliancy" (February 2, 1886, 1). The arches stood at Third and Cedar, Fourth and Sibley, and Seventh and Minnesota streets.

The parade of 1886 added ice sculpture to the wooden sidewalks. Figures such as an Indian on horseback or a snowshoe-holding marcher stood in front of shops much as the fiberglass figures of Snoopy, Charlie Brown and Lucy have done in recent summers.

Even more ice sculpture was on view the following year. An Ice King made from ice sat on a twenty-four-foot high pedestal in Bridge Square, looking down Third street (now Kellogg Boulevard). A standing ice polar bear was on Wabasha street, a musk ox further up Third street, and a gigantic snowshoe faced West St. Paul. Although parade routes seemed to change every year, decorating the streets where the parade passed was always important. After 1937 parades included one unique destination: they passed through the St. Paul auditorium where viewers could watch in warmer comfort.

The first parade, on January 15, 1886, was for the ceremonial beginning of Ice Palace construction. The walls of the central tower actually stood over thirty feet above the foundation, but on this day Miss Clemmie Finch, the daughter of the 1886 Carnival President, poured water from a silver pitcher over the ice blocks sent by the citizens of Fargo and Stillwater. Speeches and band music marked the event, which was watched by Governor Lucius Hubbard, Mayor Edmund Rice of St. Paul and Mayor John Pillsbury of Minneapolis (*St. Paul Daily Globe*, January 15, 1886, 1). Two weeks later, on February first, the Governor of Minnesota and the Mayor of St. Paul led the way to the Ice Palace for the ceremonial opening. The third day was the Grande Day parade led by Borealis Rex, going from City Hall to the Ice Palace. This parade included the sports clubs, marching on foot. On the following day horse-drawn equipages paraded. The toboggan clubs marched on the fifth day followed by a parade of the Eskimo dog trains and Sioux Indians the sixth day. The masquerade parade took place on the eighth day of Carnival, and on the next to last evening of the Carnival came the storming of the Ice Palace by Union veterans of the Grand Army of the Republic, as well as by the toboggan and snowshoe clubs. The grand finale was the Torchlight procession at eight o'clock in the evening.

The masquerade parade was organized by the German community, presided over by Prince and Princess Carnival, and supervised by Peter Giesen. A prize was offered for the "most farcical turnout" which, from the list, may have been hard to determine. The parade began at the Athenaeum on Exchange street. The Athenaeum was a combination concert hall and theater for the German community until it burned down in May of 1886. The parade was led by mounted policemen, followed by George Siebert's Great Western band, carriages carrying costumed personifications of George Washington and his staff, colonial ladies, Spanish gentlemen, Germania, Columbia, Don Quixote and Sancho Panza, the Carnival hussars and ice bears, the Sons of Hermann (a fraternal group) and, in conclusion, the First Regimental Band (*St. Paul Daily Globe*, February 9, 1886). A few wagons entered seemed to have escaped from an Industrial parade, but on the whole the masquerade parade provided theatrical and comic relief.

One parade given special attention in the 1880s was that of the equipages, or horse-drawn carriages. In that era many St. Paul families owned carriages and were willing to assemble, for example, every Thursday afternoon (in 1887) for a drive from Seven Corners east through the downtown to the Ice Palace. Those who had unusual cutters or sleighs were encouraged to participate and decorate horses and carriages with plumes and ribbons. As one reporter described it:

> There were hundreds of fine turnouts, sleighs of all styles, drawn by one, two, three, four or more horses, harnessed two or three abreast, tandem or otherwise. All were decorated with gaily colored plumes on the heads and saddles of the animals and on the dashboards of the sleighs, while garlands of evergreen were entwined about the horses and knots of ribbons were tied here and there about the harness... Nearly every sleigh contained several ladies and many were driven by the ladies themselves...Strangers in the city were delighted as well as astonished to see that St. Paul's boast of having the largest number of winter turnouts of any city in the country was so easily demonstrated (St. Paul Daily Globe, January 21, 1887).

Later carnivals would always schedule two parades: the day or Grande and the evening or Torchlight. Some parades marched to an Ice Palace, depending on its location, but not when it stood in the more distant city parks such as Como, Phalen, or Highland. After construction of Interstate 94 cut a deep swath through St. Paul, parades no longer included the Capitol Mall, but confined their routes to the area between Mears and Rice Parks.

The second and third Carnivals had two other unusual parades. One was for dogs and the other, the Industrial Parade, was for St. Paul businesses. "The Finest display of dogs ever seen in the Northwest" began with a display of "indescribable tumult" before the dogs marched out on their parade route. The canine corps was preceded by mounted policemen, the Metropolitan Band and various toboggan club members. Then came 175 dogs, beginning with Ulmers (German boar hounds), followed by greyhounds, Irish setters, fox terriers and last, definitely least, dachshunds. The finest animals, wrote the reporter, were Don Cesar and Minka, the large Ulmer dogs; most numerous were the English setters (*St. Paul and Minneapolis Pioneer Press*, January 28, 1887).

When it was the turn of businesses to parade their wares, "no one ever saw such a crowd in Third Street," wrote the *Daily Globe*. "Every business, industry and trade appeared in line and proved far more interesting and instructive than any Mardi Gras or street festival on record. There were butchers, bakers, brewers, foundries, grocers, presses, boilers, school rooms, stationery stores, organs and every branch of trade one would well imagine… A grand showing was made by the fire department and every branch of city service. The old settlers, in one immense wagon, appeared as statues of the prosperity of a great city and on every hand were received with great favor. The Knights of the Grip formed a pretty and pleasing line… It was a great exhibit of wealth, prosperity and progress… (*St. Paul Daily Globe*, February 2, 1888).

City services were represented by the fire department, street and sewer departments (some of the night brigade in yellow oilskins), and street sweepers. They were followed by eight tandems pulling one snow plow each, and seventy snow carts in double file. The wholesale division featured floats and turnouts loaded with tea, coffee and tobacco tubs (Allen, Moon & Company); toboggans and hunting outfits (M. F. Kennedy); "a long laboratory on runners, with long white bearded chemists mixing drugs" (Noyes Bros. & Cutler); four wagon-loads of fruit (Cummings & Fillebrown); Cleopatra's barge with ancient oarsmen (the Detroit Stove Works); and two men playing billiards who stood on the Standard Billiard Hall float.

Men made barrels and casks on the St. Paul Barrel company's float and sat in splendor on a suite of parlor furniture from A. Volk. Stonecutters carved a marble slab (Lauer Bros.) and the Ryan Hotel put a replica of its barbershop on a float. All in all it was an amazing and fascinating display.

In 1917 three major parades took place with firm rules established. The day parade was only for the marching clubs. Each of them was requested

Decorated vehicle from the 1917 parade.

The 1916 Dragon Float of the Business and Professional Men's Association. Courtesy of the J. J. Hill Library.

"The Colossus of Roads," and the 1928 Northern Pacific Railroad float. Courtesy of the Minnesota Historical Society.

to elect a queen and to devise a way for her to be in the parade but not to march. This meant using a sedan chair, a sled, or some other conveyance which could be pulled or carried. Mini toboggans and sleighs were common, but the queen chosen for the C. R. Gotzian Shoe Company rode in a giant shoe. Evening parade rules specified that every member of a marching club had to carry a lighted torch or light of some kind or the club could not participate.

Decorated vehicles were another innovation among the 1917 parades. Paper or canvas flowers or striped patterned sheets transformed the touring cars into small floats. Some clubs completely covered the car to create figures, such as the dragon of the Business and Professional Men's Club.

The Industrial Parade, with each wagon displaying the tools of a trade or the wares of a company, disappeared from Carnival schedules after 1917. Companies continued to sponsor

floats, but were required, instead, to use the Carnival theme for the float design.

While horses (or moose, oxen, and elk) were once used to pull the wagons and chariots, after the motorized float became routine horses were no longer needed. They did, however, continue to perform in parades. The Hook-'em-Cows horse patrol and the various military or police units could be seen in Carnival parades before World War II. Guests for both parades and performances during these years included the Lord Strathcona Horse, a mounted Canadian unit (1939), and the Shriners' White Horse Troop from Sioux City, Iowa (1940).

History changed two Carnivals in their duration and participation. The first time was in 1918. The United States was at war, but St. Paul decided to have a one-day Carnival at Fort Snelling. Carnival clubs and royalty put on a pageant, and, wearing their rainbow uniforms, took part in ice baseball, pushball, ski-joring, skating and tobogganing. There was only one parade – a night one – for the city and a convention of Minnesota advertising executives (*St. Paul Pioneer Press*, January 13 and 22, 1918).

In 1943 the Carnival-time was again transformed. "St. Paul Goes to War" was the theme for a four-day program involving both the armed services and the home front workers. Army guns and trucks, line after line of soldiers, followed by the Navy, the Marines, and then the Minnesota National Guard all formed the procession of 25,000 civilians and military marchers. Jeeps pulled floats, anti-tank weapons and anti-aircraft units rolled past, and floats carried candidates for "Miss Freedom," clad in work clothes (*St. Paul Pioneer Press*, January 27 and 30, 1943).

1937 was a big year for the Carnival. The winter celebration was beginning again so the palace, parade, and pageantry should all be over-size and they were. Even the crowd watching what some later described as "the parade from hell" was one of the largest to witness a Carnival parade. Its size meant that marchers and floats had great difficulty navigating the streets and some units never passed the reviewing stand at all.

In New York City Macy's department store employees participated in a Thanksgiving Day parade in 1924 with floats, marching bands and zoo animals. In 1927 giant helium filled balloons were added and it was the Macy's balloons which St. Paul parade planners decided would make their parade different in 1937. Forty-two bal-loons were ordered from Philadelphia, including Felix the Cat, Mickey Mouse, an elephant, toy soldier, goblins, a forty-two foot long hippopota-mus, and, largest of all, an eighty-two-foot long dragon. None would bobble and float above the crowd as Macy's balloons always seemed to do. In St. Paul each balloon was tethered to a wheeled base, guided along by men and boys dressed as clowns. Floodlights mounted on parade route buildings cast weird shadows as what were termed "grotesque" balloons rolled along in the Torchlight parade.

In the 1930s big became beautiful in Minnesota, affecting both outdoor sculpture and parades. Bemidji began its winter carnival in 1937, centering festivities around an eighteen-foot tall concrete sculpture of Paul Bunyan. St. Paul recognized the popularity of the giant log-ger by devoting one Carnival parade to him. The star of the show was Paul's faithful friend, Babe the Blue Ox, who rode in the parade on the top of a truck. Smoke came through his nostrils so he appeared appropriately fierce. Babe had a hard time returning home. One horn drooped, his sides buckled, and he needed serious repairs, all

caused by the rough roads (*St. Paul Pioneer Press,* February 3, 1937, 4).

In 1938 Paul's prowess as a hunter was shown in the giant gun and Black Duck which jour-neyed from the town of Blackduck to the Winter Carnival. The float on which they rode was built on a former Forest Service truck. The Black Duck and Paul Bunyan's gun were set on top of sleigh runners on the float. Behind them came a cutter in which the Blackduck carnival queen rode. First the float appeared in the Bemidji win-ter carnival, then it was taken to Minneapolis for a weeklong display in a Dayton's ground floor window, and finally came its appearance in St. Paul. As a newspaper report noted:

> *Considerable difficulty had been experience by the Blackduck group in making arrange-ments and in getting the huge float out of the Auditorium basement where it had to be assembled. They found the doors were not made wide enough nor high enough for Paul Bunyan's huge relics and had to be satisfied with bringing up the rear of the parade instead of the coveted position in the first division which had been awarded by parade officials. This was due mainly because the duck was too high to leave the Auditorium by the exit pro-vided and had to be turned around and driven back through the main entrance after making its official entry to the Auditorium (*Blackduck American, *February 2, 1938).*

While there were other Paul Bunyan Winter Carnival parades in St. Paul after 1938, the Black Duck and the Blue Ox no longer attended.

The Victory parade, held in 1946 after the second World War had ended, was another giant yet very happy occasion. The troops had returned so they marched and, as Gareth Hiebert who was part of that parade recalled, "not in line, not in cadence," and not always in uniform. They were home and the war was over. As they came down the hill past the Cathedral parade watchers often welcomed them with beer and enthusiasm. The parade became more and more spirited as it passed by.

A new route for a daytime parade was pioneered in the 1980s when bands, bellringers, clowns, the Aqua Jesters, and the Hamm's bear took a two and one-half mile trek through the skyways, from the Wabasha Court to the Radisson hotel. Grand Marshal in 1982 was former Viking football player Bob Lurtsema.

Drawing of the boat-shaped royal float and its polar bear guards in the 1886 parade.

Skyways, especially the portions over streets, would become favored indoor viewing places for parades. While viewers would miss the sounds, music and interaction of the parade, they did stay warm.

One important, modern change from the parades of the past involves giveaways. In the great Industrial Parade of 1888 many wagons carried workers making products and sometimes handing out samples. For example, Peterman's Viennese bakery had "white-aproned chaps" who tossed buns right and left to the crowd (*St. Paul Daily Globe*, February 2, 1888). Concerns over accidents led to strict guidelines on such generosity. Now nobody is permitted to throw things from a float, at the risk of being immediately banished from the parade. Marchers who walk near the curb still can distribute souvenirs, however, but not those who ride.

Floating Down the Street

For the first Carnival the Ice King made an impressive arrival at Union Station in an ice-covered train supplied by the St. Paul, Minneapolis, and Manitoba Railroad. His majesty then switched to his ceremonial chariot, the boat-hull sleigh called the "Nightingale," which had been sent from Boston. This carved and gilded sleigh was covered with white robes and pulled by twelve white horses. On either side marched three polar bears. Later the "Nightingale" was fitted with seats so that forty members of three different children's toboggan clubs could ride in comfort in the parade.

The St. George's Snow-shoe Club's float measured twenty by thirteen feet and was drawn by six horses. J. J. Parker, who designed the float, had four tiers rise above the float platform. On each tier some of the seventy club members stood, forming a pyramid with a single man and the club emblem at the top. The *St. Paul Dispatch* considered this "the most novel and elegant feature ever displayed in a parade in the West" (February 3, 1886).

The Windsor hotel's toboggan club featured fifty-eight lovely ladies wrapped in white wolf robes riding a toboggan-shaped float, thirty feet long by ten feet wide. The color scheme was blue and white for float draperies, for the canopy like

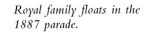

Royal family floats in the 1887 parade.

Lithograph of the Ice King sleigh in the 1887 parade.

PROCESSION OF THE ICE KING.

that on Cleopatra's famous barge, and for the ladies' uniforms. Nine horses pulled the sleigh and two polar bears walked near the front. Two large swans with blue ribbons in their beaks were mounted on the curved front of the sleigh. This production was designed by C. J. Montfort, hotel owner, and Charles Wallingford, who had worked on the street arches (*St. Paul Pioneer Press*, February 2, 1886). The Windsor float was awarded the prize in that year's competition. By 1896 the Club decided to use what remained of its prize money to purchase a sterling silver punch bowl to be given to the winning curling team. On one side of the bowl a representation of their famous float was engraved.

Statewide as well as national support was always important to the Carnival. Legend characters in the early years represented Duluth, Minneapolis, and Stillwater, as well as St. Paul. To encourage attendance marching clubs and, later, Carnival royalty, would visit other communities to invite clubs to organize and march in parades. Snow queens, fire queens, marching clubs, drill teams and floats have all come to St. Paul as a result of these invitations. In 1896 the Chisago County Rabbit Club (from Lindstrom) marched with two displays advertising sporting possibilities north of St. Paul. These were a canvas boat with a fisherman inside, and a black bass weighing 208 pounds, caught in Lindstrom lake (*St. Paul Pioneer Press*, January 22, 1896).

In the next Carnivals Borealis Rex and his principal courtiers rode in "chariots" as their floats were often called. The five used in 1887 were alike except that Borealis' was the largest. The shape of the chariot was curved in front much like that of a toboggan, while in back of the King was a curved canopy "to protect him from the Fire King." He sat on an ermine-

trimmed chair. The chariot was painted white, sprinkled with silver, its sides festooned with garlands of evergreens. Six white horses pulled Borealis' float. His Lord High Executioner, whose curious title may relate to the production of "The Mikado" then being staged in St. Paul, rode on a float drawn by a pair of moose and a single elk. The Master of the Rolls had eight Hudson Bay dogs, tandem, pulling his chariot; seven more dogs pulled the Master of the King's Bed Chamber's float; and last came the Lord High Chancellor, riding a float pulled by five Shetland ponies, four abreast and one leading. Walking alongside all five chariots was the usual guard of polar bears.

The following year there were again five "floats in the royal suite." These were designed by William Van Slyke of the Carnival committee, aided by Theodore Rank and Charles Trowbridge. The Ice King's was thirty-two feet long with the four others ranging from twenty-four to twenty-eight feet in length. The Ice King rode on a high throne with a canopy. Behind the throne was an antelope and, in front, a Rocky Mountain goat. The wood framework of each float was covered with white canvas painted in white, blue and green to resemble ice, snow and hoar frost. All of the floats were pulled by teams of milk-white horses, led by bears. The shape of each float was intended to suggest a seal, a whale, and polar bears. The harnesses were white, frosted with diamond dust, white frost plumes were placed on the horses' heads and "sweet-toned bells" jingled and jangled as they went along.

Borealis Rex and Fire King Coal had different sorts of chariots in 1896. The Ice King rode seated in a chair seemingly carved from ice, placed underneath a grotto of icicles. Drifts of snow (cotton flannel) and silver tinsel surrounded him, and blocks of ice were chairs for his courtiers. White lanterns illuminated the float, which had a standing polar bear on the prow and polar bear guards marching alongside.

The Fire King's float was basically red with touches of green and blue to suggest burning lava. Around his square cavern serpents twined themselves up the columns. Urns with flames and red lanterns served to decorate the fiery monarch's float. He was escorted by members of the Minneapolis Flambeau Club, wielding their flashing torches. Both floats were built by sign painter T. R. Wilwerscheid, and designed by Marcus Lawson, a St. Paul artist who had been designing theater sets in Boston. The Lord High Chancellor (T. W. Hugo) rode a float presented by members of the Osman Temple Shrine. This float bore a sphinx, a camel on which Chancellor Hugo sat, and Masonic emblems in "dull old Egyptian tints" (*The Daily Pioneer Press*, January 22, 1896).

Her Majesty, the Daisy Queen, rode her horse astride, as if on a bicycle (which was another symbol of the New Woman).

Great Northern Railroad float from the 1916 parade. Courtesy of the J. J. Hill Library.

The Hilex Gnomes ride in a 1949 parade. Floats often appeared, with slight modifications, in more than one parade Courtesy of Steve Shumaker.

The floats of 1916 and 1917 could certainly not match the splendor of the earlier Carnivals. What the first twentieth century parades had, in contrast, was masses of people, walking. Floats were fashioned on sleigh runners, as before, or from covered-over motorized vehicles, and there were also animal-drawn floats such as that of the Hook-'em-Cows, which was pulled by a team of oxen.

With the 1937 revival year the modern era of float-building began. No longer would floats or chariots only be animal-drawn. The motorized modern floats were "self-propelled" with trucks and later, jeeps, used to push or pull the units. Since they were no longer restricted to platforms placed on wagons, floats could be erected on shaped bases.

How to conceal or incorporate the vehicle is always a problem for the float builder. Bob Edgett of Gordon Shumaker's float-building firm recalled the year that a 3M float carried a huge pirate ship. Pulling the float was a treasure chest with "gold doubloons" and a Morris Mini-car beneath. Edgett, as the shortest member of the staff, was assigned to drive the car-in-a-chest. Parade day was bitter cold and Edgett shivered a lot especially since the treasure chest had been built with an open lid which offered no protection from the weather.

Businesses paid for the modern floats and at least some, if not all floats, were built by specialized float-building companies. Those who had designed earlier chariots were sign painters or carpenters, or carriage builders. Now with more parades and more display work, firms would become specialists. There would, of course, be exceptions. 3M employees built at least a few of the floats for their club and then there was the non-boat float of the St. Paul Yacht Club. According to James Taylor Dunn who wrote a history of that group, "The City of St. Paul" was a sternwheel boat parade float built on the base of a former Ramsey County bookmobile bus. In 1984 the Yacht Club members created it to honor sternwheel boats of the past.

The pre-World War II floats were built by Gerald V. Cannon or by the Vaughn Displays Company. That company later moved to Florida to concentrate on their work for the Orange Bowl. After World War II this left the Winter Carnival and the Minneapolis Aquatennial work to Gordon Shumaker, and his firm, initially known as Don's Displays. As display manager for Snyder Drug Stores Shumaker built floats for the three first Aquatennial parades. After serving in the Navy during World War II, he returned to Minnesota and began his firm. For many years his company would design and build a great majority of the Winter Carnival floats.

The process began with the Carnival or parade themes, which weren't always the same. In 1955, for example, the Carnival theme was "Frosty Frolic" and the parade theme was "Dreams." Five years later "The Festival of Snows" was the Carnival slogan but "Walt Disney Folk Lore" was illustrated by the floats. In 1966, fifty years after Louis Hill's "Make it a Hot One" Carnival, a reprise was considered, but fortunately rejected since that would have coincided with the massive fire at the Shumaker display company. "Festivals USA" had been planned as 1966's parade theme, but was then repeated the following year because so many of the floats had been destroyed. For 1967's "Festivals USA," floats

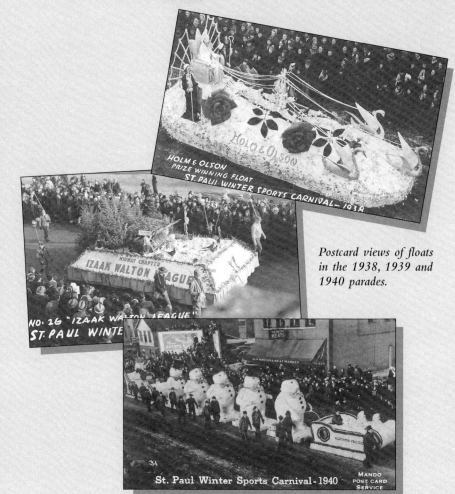

Postcard views of floats in the 1938, 1939 and 1940 parades.

Penguins and a princess in a skate ride the Farwell, Ozmun Kirk & Company float in the 1939 parade. Courtesy of the Minnesota Historical Society.

The 1948 Brown & Bigelow Company float. Courtesy of the Minnesota Historical Society.

saluted the Mardi Gras (Hi-Lex), the Veiled Prophet (Minnesota Federal Savings & Loan), and San Antonio's Fiesta Flambeau (Economics Laboratory), among others.

Once the theme had been selected, Shumaker's wife, Shirley, would sketch possible floats to be shown to various clients. The accepted sketch was the guide and blueprint from which the float would be constructed. Both she and Bob Edgett, who also worked with Shumaker, recall that each client was shown three different sketches, newly prepared, and never re-used. Often clients would request something very commercial the first time and then, after they saw what other floats were like, they would ask for something less obvious the next year.

Most Carnival parades had between fifteen and thirty floats. Some floats were new and used that year's parade theme, but a community could enter the same float celebrating its own festival more than once. Companies also used the same float, but with minor modifications, for both the Aquatennial and Winter Carnival parades. Hamm's requested what became known as "road floats," which could be folded down, covered with tarpaulins, and dispatched to other local festivals. Float designers made it simple to knock down and reassemble the floats, sending directions and diagrams along. They also arranged places for the brewery's bear to ride safely, often resting him face down on his nose. One of the road floats was the 1964 Carnival float with its rodeo theme. The bear stood, throwing his lariat, while a smaller bear rode a bucking bronco. That float appeared in the Winter Carnival, Minneapolis Aquatennial and thirty-four other civic parades during that year.

An artist's drawing was the first stage in float design. The Ice Palace, skaters, a sleigh, and toboggans recreate the 1886 Winter Carnival on this Whirlpool Corporation float in the 1964 parades. Courtesy of Steve Shumaker.

The Hamm's bear that rode on the road floats was made of fiberglass or Celastic, but for many years the Shumakers also made the Bear plush costumes worn by marchers for the brewery.

One of the most elaborate Hamm's floats was built for the Carnival's seventy-fifth anniversary in 1961. An ice castle with the brewery bear, and with beavers working near it, towed the longer throne unit of the float. Standing candelabras flanked the covered throne. Singer Dorothy Collins, wearing a velvet robe covered with rhinestones, rode on the float (*St. Paul Pioneer Press*, January 29, 1961). Another special float for 1961 was built for the Tournament of Roses by Gordon Shumaker's firm. A giant rose and a golden coach pulled by a horse on a football field represented the California festival in the St. Paul parades.

The theme of the 1973 Aquatennial parade was "Seas of Antiquity." Grain Belt's Trojan Horse made its first appearance in that parade, and then appeared in the 1974 Winter Carnival parades. Artist's sketch for float courtesy of Steve Shumaker.

A handcrafted mermaid rode on this Grain Belt float in both the Aquatennial and Winter Carnival parades of 1971 and 1972. Artist's sketch for float courtesy of Steve Shumaker.

Dorothy Moore, Hamm's princess, rides the brewery's Oktoberfest float in the 1964 Carnival parade. Courtesy of J. E. Reische.

The Hamm's bear rides the "Discovery of America" float during the snowy 1976 Torchlight Parade.

Building a float usually took weeks although construction crews often had only days to finish their work. Once the Grande Day Parade had ended, floats went back to the Shumaker shop to have lighting attached for the Torchlight Parade, traditionally held several days later.

In 1963 the Shumaker firm built nineteen of the twenty-one floats that appeared in Winter Carnival parades. Three years later, when the firm was located in northeast Minneapolis, seventeen floats were virtually complete when a tragedy occurred. A four-alarm fire raged through the building, destroying those floats that had been finished and were still parked inside. Floats standing outside suffered water damage, but could be repaired. Carnival officials decided to cancel the Torchlight Parade, while postponing the Grande Day event for several days. Shumaker and his staff moved into the St. Paul Auditorium's exhibition hall to salvage the parade. Dayton's donated materials and, with the help of dozens of volunteers, enough floats were re-built to put on a good show (*St. Paul Dispatch* and *St. Paul Pioneer Press*, January 24, 1966).

Test sheet of possible
float shapes, drawn by
Bob Edgett. Designs
at the upper right and
bottom center were
used for Albrecht Fur
Company floats. Courtesy
of Steve Shumaker

Fire is always a danger in the float business, despite an emphasis on fire resistant or retardant materials. In 1968 a fifty-foot long multicolored dragon built as a Dayton's entry began acting like a dragon should by belching real flames as it rolled along. Fortunately someone rushed out from a nearby store with a fire extinguisher to put out the fire before the fire department could respond. The flames were caused by a malfunc-

tioning fogging machine (*St. Paul Pioneer Press*, January 28, 1968). Decorations on the *Pioneer Press Dispatch* float caught fire as the parade began in 1952. The newspaper's princess finished the parade riding on a delivery truck.

During the years that Carnival parades passed through the Auditorium ramp and door dimensions affected the size of the floats. Floats could not be higher than $11\frac{1}{2}$ feet, wider than nine feet, or lower than sixteen inches off the ground to enable them to ride up the ramp and into the hall. Any floats that did not meet these guidelines had to exit the same door they entered, as the Black Duck float did in 1937.

Float-building materials included wood and something called Celastic which Shumaker began using in 1952. This was a celluloid impregnated cotton that was dipped in acetone, shaped over a mold covered with tin foil, dried, and then cut apart. The sections would then be assembled, sanded, and painted. Celastic was both lighter and stronger than papier-mâché, and thus very useful for the float builder (*St. Paul Pioneer Press*, January 21, 1952). Shirley Shumaker recalled using Celastic to make a mold of the "Father of the Waters" statue in the Minneapolis city hall. The figure was the centerpiece for the City and County Public Employees float in the 1952 parade.

Shumaker designed over 600 floats in his years of working with the Winter Carnival. In addition, his firm created many of Minnesota's famous outdoor fiberglass statues, including Smokey the Bear, Big Ole the Viking, and the Fairchild Gopher at the State Fairgrounds. Shumaker's last float was a giant telephone for A. T. & T. in 1995.

Marching Together

While a few of the marching clubs of the earliest Winter Carnival parades had been organized before 1886, most had not. Some apparently met in January of 1886, chose a club name, yell, and uniform, all barely in time to participate in the first Carnival's activities. Some called themselves "toboggan clubs," while others were "skating clubs" or "snowshoe clubs." In the early parades club members sometimes carried their toboggans and marched wearing skis or snowshoes. Newspapers reported on the establishment of these new clubs, their officers, and uniforms, noting that, for example, the Union Club (with a membership of thirty-five men and twenty ladies) had organized on January twenty-second. As uniforms they wore a scarlet cap, white jacket, blue knee pants, black leggings and a white sash. Another new group was the Ice Bear Club. Its members wore white canvas suits with black masks over their faces. As they marched they fired volleys overhead from their double-barreled shotguns.

After 1900 most of the early sports groups had ceased to meet, ending their activities just as the Carnival itself did. Only the Nushka Club was apparently able to make the transition to life as a social group, and then as an in-town golf club.

The 1880s clubs seemed to be formed by friends or neighborhood acquaintances. When Louis W. Hill sought marching groups in 1916 new clubs had to be started and their genesis was the workplace. Businesses, small and large, sponsored marching clubs. Their purpose was to take part in the parades and any other Carnival activities. By far the largest contingent came from employees of Louis Hill's Great Northern Railroad, both locally and further west. Breweries, department stores, private schools, banks and clothing manufacturers all encouraged employees to join their respective marching clubs. While in 1886 parade watchers saw the Oneota, Nushka, Tippecanoe, Owls, and Wacouta clubs, in 1916 they saw the St. Paul Fire & Marine Insurance, the Elk Laundry, and the Emporium marching clubs in the parades.

The Glacier Park Marching Club in a 1917 parade.

The 1917 Marching clubs pass in review on the golf course of the Town and Country Club.

Marching clubs of 1916 and 1917 wore the famous blanket-fabric uniforms in plain colors, stripes, and plaids. They carried bells (Glacier Park), canes or quirts (the Hook-'em-Cows) and often drums. While these were not intended to be precision drill teams or drum and bugle corps, or even bands, there was definitely a "rat-a-tat-tat" as in the hundreds they marched.

One group that marched in 1916 but in far smaller numbers and perhaps less vigorously than in 1886, included the Civil War veterans. The Grand Army of the Republic had stormed Borealis' castle in 1886, but as might be expected, their ranks were far depleted thirty years later.

Other groups who appeared enthusiastically in the early years and didn't return were the Knights of the Grip or traveling salesmen and the Saloonkeepers. As an organization the Knights of the Grip had marchers in the Villard parade. Each Knight wore a long linen duster, Panama straw hat, and carried a black leather gripsack, and a palm leaf fan. They also had a club yell: "One, two, three, g-r-i-p, grip!" and some pertinent songs. They had practiced marching, so when "present arms" was commanded, each man would put his fan in front of his face, while at "guard rest" every gripsack would be turned on end and its owner would sit on it (*St. Paul Daily Globe*, February 3, 1886, 4). Marching with them was the Mankato cornet band. St. Paul was a jobbing center with its salesmen covering the Upper Midwest as their territory. Carnival committees encouraged salesmen to carry Carnival brochures and posters, spreading the word as they made their customer rounds. Louis Hill hoped they would wear Carnival costumes when they traveled, and some indeed may have done so. Lithographs of the Knights of the Grip in their group costume appeared in magazine coverage of the 1886 Carnival, but the traveling men did not appear in the 1916 or 1917 parades.

The Saloonkeepers formed their toboggan club in 1886. As the *Globe* reported, their uniform was easy and quick to put on. With aprons over their trousers, cambric coats, tall silk hats (or "tiles"), black fur earmuffs and red roses in their lapels, they were unmistakable. The Saloonkeepers, strong as an occupation before 1900, were facing temperance foes in 1916 so understandably they did not march.

Another activity that appeared at the very beginning and still is part of Carnival parades is blanket-bouncing. In 1886 the St. George's Snow-Shoe Club may have been the first group to bounce anybody. Supposedly related to an Eskimo sport which helped hunters spot distant herds or prey, groups that "bounced" carried a

The bouncing girl soars as high as the skyway in the 1983 Grande Day Parade.

twelve foot in diameter canvas. Holding this canvas about three feet above the ground, the circle of fifteen to eighteen bouncers (or, pullers) would grip the canvas tightly as they bounced their "victim" as high as thirty feet in the air. Men, often bystanders, were usually selected to be bouncing victims in the 1880s. Reactions, according to the newspapers were definitely mixed. Some "victims" took being bounced with good humor while others were angered and considered it a custom which should be banned as a nuisance. On one side of the Columbia club's bouncing blanket were the words: "United we stand; capsized you fall." In the 1916 and 1917 Carnivals the Great Northern, Glacier Park, and Commercial Clubs all "bounced."

In 1937 the St. Paul Athletic Club became the official blanket bouncers, with a designated "bounce girl." Delores Weldon had that job for four seasons, but in 1951 she retired. Harold Theisen of the St. Paul Athletic Club staff then said, "we want a woman who isn't afraid of wires and branches, looks good, and is good-natured." The reference to branches is significant, according to Karen Vento, a former bouncing girl, because when girls bounce near a tree they like to come down with a leaf as a souvenir. Audrey Leitch, a farmer's wife and mother of six, was selected for the job (St. Paul Pioneer Press, January 20, 1952).

When the Athletic Club closed in 1991, bouncing the ladies was taken on by a new group, named "The St. Paul Bouncing Team." This team had its own logo, uniform, and from time to time issued its own buttons, once with the slogan "Throwing Up since 1886." Another year the team's Carnival buttons were numbered, but all bore the same number, "36."

After tryouts, bouncing girls are recruited for a three-year stint. Karen Vento says bouncing "feels like being shot from a cannon. You're high for the rest of the day." A bouncing girl usually is young, weighs no more than 115 pounds, and is graceful but strong as she soars and falls. While it seems so effortless, bouncing for both the girls and the blanket holders is strenuous. For this reason substitute team members take turns being bouncers in a parade.

The blanket, despite being round, has leather grips on corners for the men to hold. The strongest man on the team is the brakeman, who

signals halt to a bounce. The bouncing girl runs and jumps onto the blanket opposite the brakeman, through the "door" created when the blanket is lowered. The men who stand on each side of the door are the "callers" who will yell "Ready, Begin, 1 – 2, Up She Goes!" Up she will go as often as three times per city block during a parade, depending on the crowd and perhaps the presence of television cameras. The St. Paul Bouncing Team appears in other local parades such as St. Paul's Cinco de Mayo and Grand Old Days, and out-of-town events such as Northfield's Defeat of Jesse James Days.

Louis Hill suggested to many groups in St. Paul that they organize marching clubs. In South St. Paul the message reached men in the stockyards industry and the Hook-'em-Cows were born. In 1916 and 1917 they marched, in maroon and white uniforms. Their badges and hats had a small bell with the words "Eat More Meat." Waving canes and wearing special club badges with tiny cowbells, they accompanied their queen who rode in a sleigh pulled by Arabian horses. Like many other clubs of the time the Hook-'em-Cows went inactive after those Carnivals.

When the call for interest in the 1937 Carnival came, the Hook-'em-Cows were ready to join and ride again. Membership grew to almost 2,000. There were now a band, a horse patrol, and a drum corps led by Sam Buron, the country's only Drum Major on horseback, riding his jet black horse. The Hook-'em-Cows went to festivals at New Ulm, Stillwater, White Bear Lake, Henderson and Pine Island, but some of the best known events occurred during the pre-World War II Carnivals. The Hook-'em-Cows joined other horse patrols in several carnival rodeos. They even invited the Carnival-

Marching units of the 1938 Carnival parade on Kellogg Boulevard. Viewers watch from the roof of the Women's City Club at the lower right. Courtesy of the J. J. Hill Library.

John T. Flanagan, age 11, in his 1917 Hook-'em-Cow uniform, standing in front of the Hamm's Brewing Company aerosled. Courtesy of the author.

Louis W. Hill, Sr., and the King's Hussars march on Summit Avenue in the 1938 parade.

The Hilex Gnomes march in the 1949 parade. Note the tether connecting Hi and Lex. Courtesy of the Minnesota Historical Society.

In 2001 the sad remnants of the Hilex Gnomes rest near a wall. Courtesy of Bill Wald.

goers to their hometown. Fifteen thousand people crossed the Mississippi river to march, use the toboggan slide, and eat 1,500 gallons of booya (*Time* magazine called it "stew"), served in Hook-'em-Cow-marked pails. The party was in the parking lot adjoining the slide. When Hook-'em-Cow riders passed the State Capitol in 1937 they were joined by member (and then Governor) Harold E. Stassen. Although Hook-'em-Cows rode in at least one post war parade (in 1946), after that interest waned and South St. Paul's Carnival club apparently disbanded.

The Hilex Gnomes joined the Carnival parades beginning in 1939. At first there were only a few, but the Hilex troop eventually numbered more than thirty fiberglass oversized heads. The first Gnomes were fashioned out of papier-mâché in 1939 by Asa and Gene Eldredge, founders of the Hilex Company. A more durable fiberglass contingent joined the Hilex troop of Gnomes for the 1948 parades. Their cheerful features were painted on their faces with holes pierced in the eyes and mouths. Long, floppy cloth arms dangled from their shoulders. The two largest Gnomes, "Hi" and "Lex," had limited sight and turning ability so a "reinsmaster" was always assigned to direct them with attached guidelines. At first the Gnome costumes were worn by Hilex employees. But since 1940 Boy Scouts from Troop 13, sponsored by St. Columba's Catholic Church, have marched as Gnomes, wearing red or blue sweat pants under their Gnome costumes.

In January 2001, word was out that the Winter Carnival and Saint Paul were about to be Gnome-less. *Pioneer Press* columnist Don Boxmeyer reported that the new, absentee owners of Hilex, the KIK Corporation of Toronto, Canada, had sent a vice president for efficiency to

inspect the Hilex warehouse. He ordered that the storage areas be cleaned out and the Gnomes destroyed. Some were actually sawed into bits, but one employee spirited away a small family of nine, including their leaders, "Hi" and "Lex." These Gnomes were then bought by an antiques dealer, Wally Wescott (*St. Paul Pioneer Press*, January 5, 2001, B1).

The Gnome story didn't end there. A letter to the KIK Corporation brought a promise and an apology from David Cynamon, Chairman and CEO of KIK International. He was sorry that Gnomes had been destroyed, and promised to retrieve any that remained so that the company could continue to participate in future carnivals. He even sent a check to the Boy Scouts, continuing the annual $500 company donation (Letters dated January 5 and 10, 2001, in the files of Troop 13, St. Columba's Church). According to Bill Wald, Gnomes coordinator, the Gnomes'

The Drum and Bugle Corps of St. Paul Fire and Marine Insurance Company marches in the 1947 parade. Courtesy of Tom Swain.

But the heyday for drill teams and drum corps, however, came later. Drum corps, representing wholesalers, department stores, banks, and the railroads all entered Carnival parades after 1937. Some, according to Doug Wetherby of the Northernaires, such as the Burlington Railroad and the Field-Schlick department store, were all-girl units. The Gopher Elks drum and bugle corps was an all-black group sponsored by Peters Meat Products Company. Especially well-known were the marching units affiliated with veterans' posts and sponsored by two St. Paul breweries: Hamm's and Schmidt's. These were the Northernaires and the Indians. The Indians began in 1921 as the drum corps of American Legion Post 8, and first marched in a Memorial Day parade. By the mid-1930s the Jacob Schmidt Brewing Company was their sponsor and their uniforms, previously military, were modeled on Chippewa men's wear made by an Indian woman from Mankato. When the Schmidt brewery was sold to a Detroit company, the drum and bugle corps became the Pfeiffer Indians, until the Hamm Brewing Company took over sponsorship in 1961. By that time non-Indians could no longer possess eagle feathers in headdresses, so the eagle feathers were replaced with dyed turkey feathers. According to Bob Sheild, who worked at Hamm's at that time, the eagle feathers were donated to the Bureau of Indian Affairs. The Hamm's Indians were always seen in Aquatennial and Winter Carnival parades, often winning top honors in both. In 1965 the Indians led the way for the Winter Carnival float in the Tournament of Roses parade. Another frequent assignment was to march in the Queen's Coronation festivities in the St. Paul auditorium.

The business manager for the Indians was Gordon Shumaker, whose firm designed

record as one of the Carnival's oldest marching units will continue, since the "Gnomecide," as Father Dan Conlin, pastor of St. Columba's, described it, was prevented.

From the photographs in *The Official Souvenir View Book* it is clear that most of the business-sponsored marching clubs of the 1916-1917 Carnivals carried drums. Some, like the Golden Rule Department Store, Degree of Honor building, Lindeke Warner & Sons, Farwell Ozmun Kirk, and especially the large Glacier Park Club, had marching bands. Most clubs were led by drum majors and carried banners. The only complete exception was the Gargoyle Club. The architects who formed this group costumed themselves and marched as a twenty-five section dragon.

Coronation sets, and over 600 floats for the Winter Carnival parades. His sister, Betty Kaufer, later had the task of keeping the Indian costumes in good repair. Her husband was the drum major for the Schmidt's Indians.

The East Side Drum Corps started in 1929 and acquired sponsorship from Hamm's in 1934. It was known as the Northernaires from 1954 until the group ceased to exist in 1960. They wore a patriotic uniform of white-fringed goatskin jackets and white shirts, red ties, royal blue pants, and frontier-style hats. Like the Indians, the Northernaires marched in the Carnival parades, participated in Coronation pageantry, and won their share of prizes.

High-stepping her way into Carnival history a drum majorette made her first and only appearance on a button in 1941. Drum majorettes had been leading marching bands and drill teams since the 1937 Carnival. Increasingly, advertising, movies and magazines featured drum majorettes. A *Life* magazine cover in 1938 emphasized the growing interest in drum majorettes. With more girls interested in the baton twirling tricks and routines, contests and competitions began. The first national drum majorette competition was held at the 1941 Winter Carnival. The winner, Patty Philippi, led the Hamm's Northernaires before leaving to join the Ice Capades as a figure skater. One of her routines on ice featured flaming batons. Until 1970 drum majorette championships were a part of the Winter Carnival schedule, usually ending in performances called Musical Jamborees, held before large audiences in the St. Paul auditorium.

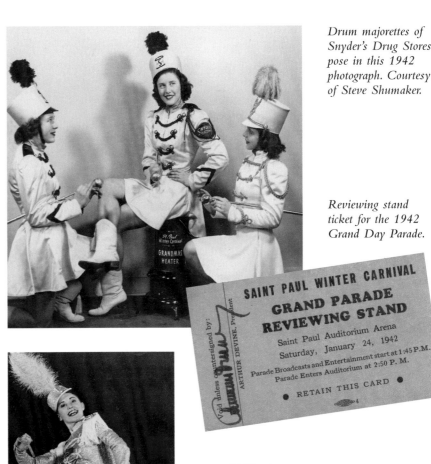

Drum majorettes of Snyder's Drug Stores pose in this 1942 photograph. Courtesy of Steve Shumaker.

Reviewing stand ticket for the 1942 Grand Day Parade.

Patty Phillippi won the first Winter Carnival majorette contest in 1941, and then toured as a skater in the 1952 Ice Capades. Courtesy of Doug Wetherby.

OFFICIAL
SOUVENIR
VIEW BOOK

St. Paul Outdoor
Sports Carnival
Jan. 27 - Feb 3RD 191_

MADE IT A HOTTER O_

Souvenirs, Publicity and Memories

5

Promoting and documenting the Winter Carnival has been a task enthusiastically taken on by St. Paul's newspapers, and later by newsreels, radio and television. George Thompson, publisher of the *St. Paul Dispatch*, has been called "the father of the Winter Carnival." It was Thompson who felt the city needed to respond to the perceived slur (the Siberian remark) by Eastern journalists and take another step in the rivalry with its sister city, Minneapolis, by launching a carnival in competition with Minneapolis' giant expositions of the 1880s and 1890s. His newspaper produced an annual pre-Carnival special edition filled with stories about forthcoming events, illustrated with fine line drawings and with a handsome color lithograph on the cover.

The *Pioneer Press, Dispatch, Globe, Daily News* and the German-language *Die Volkszeitung* carried daily front page articles and columns of news about sports, parades and the ice palaces of each Carnival. Coverage of the early Winter Carnivals could also be found in the pages of *The Northwest Magazine* as well as in the national magazines, *Harper's Weekly* and *Frank Leslie's Illustrated Monthly.*

1886 Souvenir booklet. Courtesy of John Meyers.

Advertisement for the 1888 Carnival.

Photographs taken in St. Paul by C. A. Zimmerman and Truman Ingersoll appeared often in stereopticon format and were reproduced in newspapers and magazines as engravings or lithographs. Posters were reduced to postcard size and photographic postcards of palaces and parades were mailed by the thousands. The *St. Paul and Minneapolis Pioneer Press* reported that "It is getting to be quite the fashion among businessmen to have printed a cut of the ice palace on their envelopes" (January 24, 1886, 4).

By the time of the 1916 and 1917 Carnivals newspaper coverage in both St. Paul and in Minneapolis was to be expected, but the presence of newsreel cameramen was quite new. The Carnival managers could speak proudly of publicity generated by showings of the films of the pageant, parades and sporting events throughout the country. Photographers for the Camera Art firm of St. Paul served as "official" photographers for both Louis Hill Carnivals. Their trademarks appear in both the 1916 and 1917 souvenir books.

In a letter to Louis Hill in the summer of 1916 Hugo E. Hermann of the Carnival Publishing Company noted that the press run for the Carnival's *Deluxe Souvenir View Book* (1916) was 10,000 copies. The books were selling (exclusively to the marching clubs at that point) at the rate of 250 copies per day. The cover of the book used, with permission, Louis Moen's Carnival Girl poster (Letter of Hugo E. Hermann to Louis W. Hill, Sr., July 8, 1916, Hill Papers). Despite the name of "Carnival Publishing Company," the publisher was evidently an independent entrepreneur. The next important Carnival book, Frank Madden's *Rollicking Realm of Boreas,* was originally self-published. At the same time that the Madden book appeared, a map of the Realm which he described, drawn by Rose Lyon, appeared in the *Pioneer Press* (January 22, 1939). To summarize all the events, the Winter Carnival Association published historical pamphlets marking the Carnival's seventy-fifth anniversary (in 1961) and its Centennial (in 1986).

Kenneth Wright had served as Chairman of the 1930 Midway Carnival and as its official photographer. His Northwest Photographic Studio continued to document Carnival life once the Carnival was revived in 1937. Wright's small booklets of Carnival scenes, priced at ten cents or a quarter each, appeared annually. The Erickson Studio took over as official Carnival photographer in 1960. Formal portraits of the Royal family as individuals and in a group was their assignment.

Carnival newspaper coverage included feature stories, daily schedules, photographs of the candidates for queen, and treasure hunt clues. Each year prior to the Carnival an issue of the Sunday *Pioneer Press* magazine supplement appeared with a full color photograph of the new King Boreas on its cover. Usually Boreas Rex was shown seated wearing his regal finery, but once, for variety, he posed on a stool while ice fishing. Inside the magazine were photographs of parades, royal coronations, sporting contests and often reminiscences with photographs from early Carnivals. One unusual promotion came in February 1941 when a Sunday issue of the *Pioneer Press* carried cartoon panels of "Major Hoople," "Chief Wahoo," and Jiggs and Maggie of "Bringing Up Father," all related to the Carnival.

Carnival committee members, the Knights of the Grip, and anyone else who traveled before a Carnival were asked to help with promotion. "Snow Trains" prior to World War II were part of the publicity effort. Trips for the Carnival marching clubs and the Royal Families were arranged by rail to Minnesota and nearby Wisconsin cities. For a roundtrip fare of two to

Movie newsreel photographers first appeared at the 1916 and 1917 Carnivals. Courtesy of the J. J. Hill Library.

This billboard advertising the 1916 Winter Carnival stood on Summit Avenue across from the University Club. Courtesy of the J. J. Hill Library.

Postcard advertising the 1916 Carnival.

OFFICIAL
SOUVENIR
VIEW BOOK

St. Paul Outdoor
Sports Carnival
Jan. 27-Feb 3RD 1917

"WE MADE IT A HOTTER ONE"

*Cover of the Official
Souvenir View Book for
the 1917 Carnival.*

three dollars Club members marched in parades, skied, tobogganed or skated, and then went to dinner and evening festivities. They left by train in the morning and returned in the late evening hours. A St. Cloud trip in January 1941, via the Great Northern Railroad was priced at $1.50. It was a special day and destination since Boreas Rex VII (John F. Scott) came from St. Cloud. Other Snow Train trips were arranged that year to La Crosse, Mankato, Albert Lea, and Duluth.

In addition to the printed and photographic records of Carnival events, other souvenirs abound. Buttons (described in the next part of this Chapter), posters, postcards, sheet music, programmes, trophies, poster stamps, statuettes, cigars, coffee mugs, pewter, china or armetale plates, window cards, uniform badges, club banners, and Carnival jewelry of all sorts exist, some in incredible quantities. One statement about the 1917 Carnival mentions 100,000 examples of both poster stamps and postcards already printed. Poster stamps often used the

50,000 of these oversized advertising matchbooks were ordered for the 1948 Carnival.

Cigar with a 1917 Carnival Girl wrapper.

King Boreas, ruler of the North Wind, invites you to the nation's greatest Winter Carnival in St. Paul, Minnesota

For information write to Saintpaulites Incorporated 89 East Fifth Street St. Paul 1. Minn.

COLORFUL PARADES · CORONATION PAGEANTRY · SPECTACULAR FIREWORKS · MUSICAL JAMBOREE · SPEED SKATING · SKIING CONTESTS · HOCKEY GAMES · CURLING BONSPIEL · FIGURE SKATING · QUEEN OF THE SNOWS BALL · MAJORETTE CONTEST

SEE THE GIGANTIC PALACE OF ICE

same designs developed for posters and postcards. The stamps were usually printed by Brown & Bigelow or by Greene Engraving Company, both of St. Paul. Small sheets of these stamps exist for the Carnivals of 1916 and 1917, and individually for the 1937 through 1941 prewar events. Only twenty-three of the seven-inch-high Carnival Girl plaster statuettes were sold, either plain or tinted. Other limited edition items were the purple and gold pens given by Brown & Bigelow to those attending the annual Court of Boreas luncheons held by the Midway Civic Club.

Whether anyone saved one of the publicity items from the Midway Carnival of 1929 is not known, but they were unusual. To emphasize winter sports the Midway Civic Club ordered 500 giant wood snowshoes. Said the chairman, they were "fit for Paul Bunyan." These were printed with the Carnival dates and tied to lampposts throughout the area (*St. Paul Dispatch,* January 25, 1929).

How the 1916 publicity materials would be distributed was the subject of a letter from W. R. Mills to Louis W. Hill. Mills noted that the window cards had already been placed in store windows as well as in the passenger cars of all railroad trains serving St. Paul, including the lines of the Great Northern, Northern Pacific, Omaha, Great Western, Burlington, Milwaukee, Soo, M & St. L, and Rock Island. McGill Warner, the printer, was about to deliver 1,030 cards to be hung in all Twin Cities streetcars. The postcards, continued the committee chairman, were to be distributed to clubs, hotels, stores, and the larger restaurants. Two were to be given to each of the 24,000 school children in the city, who were asked to mail the cards to out-of-town friends (Letter of W. R. Mills to Louis W. Hill, Sr., January 11, 1916. Hill Papers).

Oversized restaurant matchbook (1937) whose front image shows the 1916 Carnival Girl. Courtesy of Bob Jackson.

Publicity via the mails has long been encouraged by Winter Carnival committees. In the 1880s the entire front side of business envelopes was printed or rubber-stamped with Carnival-related information. By the time of the 1896 Carnival, local businesses were being provided with rubber stamps and stickers to apply to outgoing mail. The rubber stamps were prepared by the Northwestern Stamp Works for business firms who promised to use them. Wrote the *Pioneer Press*, "Not one refused to give the promise" (December 18, 1895, 10).

By the time of the 1917 Carnival obtaining a special postmark device for use on mail being sent from St. Paul seemed to require a Congressional impetus. By a Joint Resolution in the House of Representatives (H. J. Res. 332, 64th Congress, 2nd Sess.) the Postmaster General was authorized and directed to provide the St. Paul Postmaster with such a die. Placed next to the circular date stamp in the postmark, the text read "Outdoor Sports Carnival, Jan. 27-Feb. 3." Supporting the reasons for such authorization was the argument the Carnival would create "a great increase of incoming and outgoing mail" for the city.

Carnivals since 1937 have often provided rubber-stamped cachets for envelopes. Usually the design showed that year's Ice Palace if there was one, plus the words "Mailed at the Ice Palace."

That was precisely the case in 1940 when an actual postal station (called the "Ice Palace Branch") was located in one of the icy corner towers of the Ice Palace. In 1942 the cachet included the words "Buy Defense Bonds."

The music inspired by the Winter Carnival is described elsewhere in this chapter. Fiction based on festival events is much rarer. F. Scott Fitzgerald's short story, "The Ice Palace," takes place in a later palace modeled on the giant Ice Palace of 1887. His Southern belle character, Sally, becomes lost inside the corridors of ice. This so terrifies her that she breaks her engagement to a St. Paul man and returns to the South. Towards the end of his life Fitzgerald was asked to write about another Winter Carnival, as Jason Tanz recently noted in *The New York Times*. He and Budd Schulberg were hired by Walter Wanger, the movie producer, to research and write a script for a movie based on Dartmouth College's Carnival. The two men went, but arrived at the college so intoxicated that after a

Queen Edna Bolke with the official street lamp decoration for the 1929 Carnival. Courtesy of the Midway Chamber of Commerce.

1916 menu of the restaurant in the Hotel Saint Paul, for many years the headquarters for Carnival events. Courtesy of the Hotel Saint Paul.

The Saint Paul
IN ST. PAUL
Carnival Season
1916

short stay, their boss told them to leave. Schulberg eventually wrote the desired script, which was released as a film starring Ann Sheridan in 1939. Fitzgerald died the following year. His last novel, *The Last Tycoon*, dealt with Hollywood, not the Carnival.

Larry Millett credited Minnesota architect Cass Gilbert with creating the design of a domed Ice Palace among his Minnesota additions to the Sherlock Holmes canon. In fact, Gilbert was a member of one of the first Carnival's committees, as Bob Olsen has noted. In Millett's mystery, a murder takes place in the palace so the English detective and Dr. Watson journey to Minnesota, stay at the James J. Hill mansion, and solve another homicide.

Poetry, on the other hand, is common. Reprinted in this book is J. H. Hanson's "An Idyl on Ice." Hanson was the first Carnival's Assistant Secretary. His poem appeared as part of a small booklet distributed by the Chicago, St. Paul, Minneapolis and Omaha Railroad. Hanson's was not the only poem to appear in print on the subject of the Carnival. T. M. Newson, editor and historian, wrote a skating song entitled "U-Le-Ho-He" and a longer salute to "The Ice King and His Palace," both for the *St. Paul Daily Globe* (January 15 and 24, 1886). Charles E. Flandrau's Ode to his Queen (published in the *St. Paul Dispatch*, rather than the Globe, which he edited at the time) is memorable.

Visitors wrote about the Carnival as well. A man then staying at the St. Paul Hotel commented, in verse, to Louis W. Hill, Sr.:

Hark at the noise on the street below
The song of the wheels on the frozen snow
The Aeolian harps of the winter time
Piercing the air through frost and rhyme.

The poet was clearly enjoying the weather for he ended his poem, "The Coming Carnival," with these lines:

For winter here is a steady thing
We bow to the Queen, we bow to the King
Let Aurora soar, and Boreas rule
The wish of warm weather is the wish of a fool.

(Letter from Thomas L. Brown to Louis W. Hill, Sr., December 31, 1916, Hill Papers).

As noted previously, Louis W. Hill was inspired to respond in verse to the Carnival queens at the luncheon in his honor at the close of the 1916 Carnival. At a time when poetry appeared daily in most newspapers it was not unexpected for Carnival leaders and others to put their thoughts into rhyme. As the *St. Paul Daily Globe* editor commented, they certainly did:

The carnival is here and the weary editor opens his morning mail shudderingly, fearing lest the fresh batch of ice palace poetry he will undoubtedly receive will be even more gruesome than the last (January 18, 1887).

Medals, loving cups, and jewelry are among the many Carnival souvenirs. Both the Fire and Ice families have jewelry. The rectangular Star of Boreas bears the north wind face surrounded by a starburst design. It hangs from a red, blue, or white ribbon and was the concept of Carl Gray, Boreas Rex V, in 1947. Members of the Vulcanus family wear an Iron Cross pin which identifies their membership in the Imperial Order of Fire and Brimstone. The Queens of the Snow have worn a large snowflake on a chain engraved with their name and year as queen. More recently a pin designed by Dimitry Mogilyinski has been worn by the Queens of the Snows. It is a silver snowflake with an inset gold crown.

The Winter Carnival depends on thousands of volunteers, from those who portray the legend characters, to those who organize and staff the Carnival committees. Each year, since 1987, in memory of the 1976 North Wind Prince, someone is honored with the Sal LoBaido Volunteer Service Award. This award comes in the shape of the 1886 Ice Palace and has been given to both individuals and couples with long years of service in Winter Carnival activities. Award winners include John and Bernice Roach, William LaLonde, Richard and Helen Murphy, Robert Sheild, Gloria Shultz, Dan Muntean, Paul Mueller, Chester Schoenrock, Gerald Lanahan, Victor and Bonnie Reim, Lorraine Venaas, Bill and Gladys Godwin, Lou Collette, Gil Thoele, Denny and Mary Harris, and Dot Bentfield. The Vulcan organization, the Imperial Order of Fire and Brimstone, presents two awards to those who have helped them and the Carnival. These are the William Tobin Sampson Memorial Award (since 1976) and the King Coal Award (since 1986).

Over 700 volunteers took part in the 1986 Ice Palace project. As Charlie Hall, chairman of the 1986 Ice Palace project remembered, one of those volunteers remarked somewhat sadly that, after it was over, no one would recall the effort contributed by so many. That, Hall felt, should not be the case, so he arranged for a more permanent memorial with the title "A Labor of Love" carved on its base. The fifteen-foot-tall Vermont granite replica of the Ice Palace stands near the original Ice Palace location on the west shore of Lake Phalen, north of the Picnic Pavilion. Names of all the volunteers and contributors were sandblasted into its base, with the lettering in the style of Maya Lin's Vietnam Veterans Wall. This granite Ice Palace memorial was dedicated in November, 1987.

Button, Button— Whose is the Button?

Winter Carnival buttons serve as festival emblems, symbols of support and membership, and badges of admission. Buttons have long been

Metal buttons for the earliest Carnivals were pierced to hang from ribbons. Shown are front and rear views of 1886 and 1887 buttons.

a primary source of funding. Those who purchase buttons frequently save them and use them as the nucleus of a Winter Carnival collection.

Buttons have been prepared for almost every Winter Carnival since 1886. In addition there were buttons produced for the 1922 municipal carnival, for the 1928–1930 festivals sponsored by the Midway business community, and for the 1935 Winter Sports Week. The earliest "buttons" were dime-sized, made of stamped metal, and often pierced to hang from a triangular-shaped grosgrain pin. By the 1896 Carnival organizers spoke of having a button since it would be less "destructible" than a silk badge (*St. Paul Pioneer Press*, December 19, 1895). Since the 1920s buttons have grown larger and occasionally ribbons or bells hang beneath them. After the Second World War four "buttons" were actually pins in the shape of plastic keys. Behind the 1949 "Fun Key" was the map of the territory of Minnesota, honoring its centenary. These "Fun Keys" suggest the token which Boreas receives annually from the mayor of St. Paul.

In 1946 the Midway Civic Club had a very large Fun Key made to carry in the parade. On the key were the words "We Found It." The Club's uniform included a small fun key carried as a cane. The canes were much in demand as souvenirs.

Buttons shaped as rectangles appeared in 1995, 1996, and 1998 and in a square in 1997. Until 1999 Winter Carnival boosters purchased one button annually, but the single "official" emblem has now become a set of four, each with a different design.

Button design usually includes the name of the event, the dates, and often the theme or slogan of each year's Carnival.

WINTER CARNIVAL THEMES

1916	"Make It A Hot One"
1917	"Make It A Hotter One"
1918	"Carnival at Fort Snelling"
1922	"I Belong"
1929	"Come and Play in Midway"
1935	"Winter Sports Week"
1941	"Show Your Colors"
1942	"All Out"
1943	"St. Paul Goes to War"
1946	"Victory"
1950	"Accent On Youth"
1951	"Hot Foot to Boreas"/"Cold Shoulder To Vulcanus"
1952	"Call of The North"
1953	"Hi Neighbor"
1954	"No Time Like Snow Time"
1955	"Frosty Frolic"
1956	"Showland Of Snowland"
1957	"Winter Wizardry"
1958	"Centennial Holiday"
1959	"Cool Capers"
1960	"Festival Of Snows"
1961	"75th Anniversary"
1962	"Winter Wonderland"
1963	"Winter's A Winner"
1964	"Toys N' Snowland"
1965	"Fun N' Frolics"
1966	"Festivals U.S.A."
1967	"Sno-A-Go-Go"
1968	"Winter Holidaze"
1969	"Arctic Antics"
1970	"Mid-Winter Magic"
1971	"Snow Foolin"
1972	"Salute to Southern Hospitality"
1973	"Western Horizons"
1974	"Northern Highlights"
1975	"Eastern Heritage"
1976	"Everybody's Ice Centennial"
1977	"Windows Of Winter"
1978	"Snowflake Fantasy"
1979	"Frosty Fascinations"
1980	"Jest Fest"
1981	"Merry Ol' Times"
1982	"Family Frolics"

1983	"Wrapped Up In Winter"
1984	"Wintertainment"
1985	"Wintertainment"
1986	"Centennial"
1987	"Winternational"
1988	"Tales of Fire & Ice"
1989	"Magical Winter Kingdom"
1990	"Celebrate"
1991	"Good Neighbors" / "Good Times"
1992	"You've Got to Believe"
1993	"Treasure the Tradition"
1994	"Brrrific!"
1995	"On with the Snow"
1996	"The Great Winter Reunion"
1997	"Winter Wonderland"
1998	"The Legend Lives"
1999	"Cure the Common Cold"
2000	"The Coolest Celebration on Earth"
2001	"The Coolest Celebration on Earth"
2002	"The Coolest Celebration on Earth"
2003	"The Coolest Celebration on Earth"

Supposed to be the rarest of buttons is the 1899 – 1900 example, for years in which no Carnival was held. The Carnival girl buttons of 1916 and 1917 were designed by Louis Moen. Courtesy of Eugene DiMartino. Marching clubs, such as the Courthouse and City Hall Club, had their own buttons in 1917. The building shown is St. Paul's second city hall, which was wrecked in 1933. Courtesy of the St. Paul Public Library.

Buttons have been designed by national and local artists, sometimes selected through competition. In 1974 a former Queen of the Snows, Dorothy Arneberg Furlong, won the design competition with her sketch of a happy polar bear driving a snowmobile. Just as her snowmobiling bear referred to the Winnipeg – St. Paul races then being run, the ice skating clown of 1980 commemorated an event. The International Shrine Clown Association had its midwestern convention during Carnival that year.

For four years (1982-1985) Brown & Bigelow supplied appropriate Norman Rockwell winter scenes from their illustration archives. Brown & Bigelow staff artists Buzz Peck and John Stumpf designed Winter Carnival buttons, Peck in 1987-1988 and Stumpf in 1979. Peck's button featured four children and a snowman holding hands as they danced around a globe. They celebrate the Winternational theme of that year's Winter Carnival which was also the year that the World Trade Center opened in St. Paul. The arrangement of the figures anticipates the snowflake composition developed for the logo in 2000.

Students of Ken Lenzmeier at the St. Paul Technical Vocational Institute designed the buttons from 1972-1975. In 1990, when the cartoon character Snoopy served as parade Grand Marshal and the *Peanuts* cartoon strip was forty years old, the button showed the beagle and a snowman riding a toboggan. This design was based upon a drawing contributed by Charles Schulz. Another St. Paul-born artist, LeRoy Neiman, used fireworks over the 1887 Ice Palace for his button design. Neiman's vista of the Palace appeared first in an oil painting and then as a serigraph, both of which were sold by the St. Paul Winter Carnival Association. Neiman's image also appeared on the cover of the Winter Carnival's Centennial history booklet in 1986.

Any winter scene can be used for the Carnival button, but to date the most popular choices have been the 1880s Ice Palaces, polar bears, snowmen, and the Ice Kings. The two Carnival Girls (Irene Grayston and Mabel Looby) as drawn by Louis Moen of the Buckbee-Mears Company, appeared on the buttons of 1916 and 1917. Edna Bolke, Midway Carnival Queen in 1928, was shown on that festival's blue button. The 1999, 2001 and 2002 sets of buttons have used photographs of former Carnival participants, including a blanket bouncing girl, a Vulcan, the Hanna Coal Company princess from 1917, and a family on a toboggan.

In 2000 the Winter Carnival, working with Concept Group, Inc, introduced its "Coolest Celebration on Earth" slogan and a new logo based on kaleidoscope patterns. The logo, with four variations, appeared on the year's set of four buttons. One of the kaleidoscope views shows six snow angels, representing ethnic diversity in the city, which connected to create a snowflake. This then became the permanent Winter Carnival logo.

The 2003 set of four took the stick figures from the Winter Carnival's snowflake abstraction and set them free to become Boreas, Vulcanus, Klondike Kate, and the Queen of the Snows, each on its own button.

Since the official button raises funds for the Carnival activities, selling the button has long been an obligation of participants. In a letter sent to the 1916 Carnival marching clubs, the then button committee chairman A. H. Warren wrote:

The Carnival button must not be regarded simply as a decorative carnival emblem, but as a carnival membership and a boost for St. Paul and the Carnival.

The button entitles the wearer to free admission to the public skating rinks, all slides, the auditorium except on pageant nights, and the National Ski Tournament... The [toboggan] slides are being opened as fast as possible and will be left up after the Carnival for the use of the public. For two months the public will be furnished recreation and enjoyment. Is a dollar button asking too much? (Letter from A. H. Warren to Carnival marching clubs, 1916, SPOSA).

In 1922 every girl who entered the queen contest sponsored by the *Dispatch Pioneer Press* was expected to sell buttons. In addition to the more than 800 queen candidates, former Carnival queens and actresses from the Greenwich Village Follies cast, then performing in St. Paul, also became button vendors (*St. Paul*

The Victory Carnival at war's end emphasized the returning servicemen and women, and even had space for their names on the buttons. The Minnesota Territorial Centennial was celebrated at the 1949 Carnival with a plastic key. Courtesy of Eugene DiMartino.

A Norman Rockwell drawing appeared on the 1983 button, and LeRoy Neiman's Ice Palace painting appeared on the 1986 Centennial button. The Wind Princes have buttons identifying themselves and their business sponsors. The reclining bear with a turban is one of a series saluting world regions. The Guards and the Vulcan Krewe members often have their own buttons. Courtesy of the author.

Dispatch, January 17 and 19, 1922). In 1937, when the Winter Carnival was revived, women's groups such as the Junior League took on the civic duty of selling buttons.

For the 1928 – 1930 Midway Carnivals, the St. Paul Jaycees helped the Midway Commercial Club sell their single color, numbered buttons. These buttons, collectors say, are hard to locate. The 1928 blue button with Edna Bolke's face, was followed by a red button in 1929 and in 1930 a green button using as a design the jumping Carnival girl of 1916. Other numbered buttons were produced for the Ice Fishing contests on White Bear Lake while buttons with the names of returning veterans appeared as a welcome home gesture for the 1946 Victory Carnival.

Buttons have at least once entitled their purchasers to vote. In 1952 the Ice King declared that his Queen should be selected by the public. A button equaled one hundred votes to be cast, in ballot boxes located in downtown bank lobbies. Beverly Prazak won the vote and became 1952's Queen of the Snows.

Today a Carnival Committee, known as the King's Tax Collectors, takes primary responsibility for button sales. Their work begins when the new buttons are unveiled. The 2003 set of four buttons, for example, was displayed first at a noontime media event involving children from Roosevelt School on December 2, 2002. The set was designed by Concept Group, Inc., of St. Paul. The button still serves as a ticket of admission to Carnival events and, if registered, offers additional prize money to the lucky finder of the Treasure Hunt medallion.

The marching clubs, businesses and Carnival royalty all have sold buttons. During the second year of their five-year-commitment members of the Vulcan Krewe sell Vulcan charms (pins or bracelet charms which are miniature versions of the Vulcan's buttons). The Mardi Gras-style chains now offered with buttons are, according to Lonny Piche of the King's Tax Collectors, the latest way to wear Carnival pins. In addition to the official Winter Carnival buttons many other buttons exist, received as gifts rather than purchased. Each Boreas Rex since 1937 has handed out a button bearing his title and number ("Boreas Rex XI," for example). So does his counterpart, the King of Fire, whose buttons began appearing in 1951. Vulcan "Coming Out" buttons also exist, as do individual Krewe members' buttons. Early buttons for the Wind Princes often used the motif of their hats: cowboy, charro, or turban. Buttons for the Wind Princes now have designs which identify them, as well as their businesses or professional affiliations which are often called their "Royal Houses." Bob Sheild, East Wind Prince in 1970, was the first to use that format. His blue and white button identified his home as the Royal House of Hamm's. For Titan the first buttons in 1962 read "Prince of the Northern Lights" which was emphasized in the design. In 1976 Titan's title became "Prince of the North Wind." Klondike Kates pass out buttons each year as do the Royal Guards and, briefly, as did the Vulcanettes.

In addition to the official buttons and those for each of the Carnival characters, buttons exist for events held during the Carnival, such as the Ashes Swing (a barhopping night in St. Paul which culminates in the Count of Ashes' performance on a swing suspended from a tavern ceiling) and the Coming Out Party of the Vulcans when their identities are revealed. And finally, when Boreas and Vulcanus Rex knight individuals they often give certificates and knighting buttons to celebrate the event.

"Mr. Hamilton, treasurer of the Sioux City road, writes to the Historical Society suggesting that it make a collection of badges and other souvenirs of the first Minnesota winter carnival. The suggestion was received with favor and will probably be carried out."

~ St. Paul Daily Globe (February 3, 1886).

The tobogganing girl belongs to the 1922 Carnival. Courtesy of the author. Three buttons, for the 1928, 1929, and 1930 Midway Carnivals, are shown with the 1935 Carnival Sports Week button. Courtesy of Eugene DiMartino.

*Prewar buttons emphasized Boreas Rex and his
Fun Key. Drum majorettes were increasingly a
part of Carnival parades and national competitions
in St. Paul. Courtesy of Dot Bentfield.*

Cover of brochure containing list of events for the 1940 Carnival.

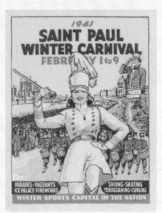

Poster stamps from the 1937 – 1942 Winter Carnivals. Courtesy of Eugene DiMartino.

"To-Bog-I-Og-I-Og-Gan" and Other Tunes

Most of this history has dealt with the visual record of the Carnival – its costumes, floats and pageantry. There is also an aural legacy in both sounds remembered but not recorded and sheet music. Had somebody been able to record early Carnivals, the music featured would have come from concerts in the Ice Palace and in ballrooms. Other sounds would derive from the explosion of fireworks, the storming of the Ice Palace by Fire King Coal and his armies, and the quieter sounds of parades: the squeak of the wagon wheels, the scrunch made by runners on sleds and sleighs, and those joyful noises made by the marchers themselves.

While their steps in moccasined feet were probably quiet, marchers nevertheless carried noisemakers and bells and were encouraged to frequently call out their club's slogan. The second By-law for the Crescent Toboggan Club in 1886 (a club to which Louis W. Hill, Sr., belonged), read:

The Club call shall be: 'Heigho, heigho, heigho, heigho, Crescent, rah, rah, rah,' and finishing with a descending mockingbird roll (Crescent Toboggan Club minute book, Hill Papers).

Many if not all the marching groups had similar yells, especially the Hook-'em-Cows club from South St. Paul. While no one captured these sounds for posterity, St. Paul composers were surely inspired by the events to create a body of Carnival music.

In 1887 a thirty-eight page Carnival music and song folio was published which included "Gloire du Carnival," "To-Bog-I-Og-I-Og-Gan," "Maids of the Carnival Waltz," "Snowshoe Polka,"

and "The Knight of the Grip and the Sample is King." This last ballad serenaded local commercial traveling salesmen who marched as a club in Carnival parades wearing long linen coats and Panama straw hats. "Cantus Carnivalis" was dedicated to the Nushka Club and "Charge of the Fire King" to his red-clad majesty. S. T. Church compiled the folio with several songs written by C. G. Titcomb, Professor Franz Stollwerk, and others. Professor Stollwerk's "Carnival March" appeared as sheet music in 1916, dedicated to the Carnival Clubs of the Northwest, with the red coated Carnival Girl on the cover.

In 1939 the Carnival board of directors chose this to be the official Winter Carnival song.

The opening verse of one 1917 Winter Carnival song, "Back to Old St. Paul," with words and music by Harley Rosso, went as follows:

"Listen folks I'm going now,
Back to Old St. Paul,
To join the shouting Hook 'em Cow
For a big carnival…"

Another opus dedicated to Louis Hill was Joseph Hezekiah Barrett's "Glacier Park Outdoor Carnival March" (1916). Most of the Minnesota works mentioned were written for either the Carnivals of the 1880s or for the 1916 – 1917 events when pageantry was being invented and needed a musical accompaniment.

Promoting the Carnival in 1937 involved billboards and posters distributed by Northwest Airlines and Northland Greyhound bus lines, as well as radio programs. Fifteen-minute broadcasts over WTCN featured Margie Garretson and C. J. Byrne playing and singing some of the Carnival

Lithographed cover of a portfolio of 1887 Winter Carnival songs. Courtesy of Bob Jackson.

Sheet music for the 1886 "Ice Palace March." Courtesy of Walt and Lynn Hedblum.

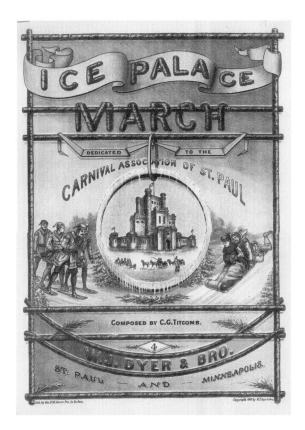

Sheet music for the 1916
"Carnival March."

1937 sheet music for
"The Spirit of the St.
Paul Winter Carnival is
Here." Courtesy of Walt
and Lynn Hedblum.

songs. By then a number of parodies and original compositions existed (*St. Paul Dispatch*, January 22, 1937, 1A). Byrne wrote new words to "The Maine Stein Song," in honor of visiting musician Rudy Vallee whose theme it was. William J. Kugler's "The Spirit of the St. Paul Winter Carnival is Here," also comes from 1937. Its sheet music has an Art Deco-style skater in the diamond format of the 1937 button.

Sheet music for a 1957 Winter Carnival march. Courtesy of Bob Jackson.

Collecting and Carnival Collections

Many of the items illustrated in this book come from private collections. Some who preserve Carnival history have been part of it as legend characters. Each of the uniformed groups asks one of its members to serve as historian so that pertinent records will be saved. Other collectors have simply become interested and sought out costumes, photographs, paper ephemera, badges, and perhaps above all, the numerous buttons. Each year several collectors have brought objects from their collections to display in Landmark Center during Carnival time.

Several St. Paul institutions have Winter Carnival collections. The largest belongs to the Minnesota Historical Society. At the History Center visitors can read all local newspapers on microfilm and consult any printed items, or films and photographs, in the library. Viewing the costumes and other three-dimensional objects requires making an appointment with the curator in charge. Other collections of Winter Carnival materials are at the St. Paul Public Library, at the Ramsey County Historical Society, and in the Louis W. Hill, Sr. collection at the James J. Hill Library. Artifacts relating to the Hook-'em-Cows are in the Dakota County Historical Society in South Saint Paul. During Carnival weeks many of these museums display items from their Winter Carnival collections.

The Winter Carnival Programme

6

Each year the Winter Carnival committees plan the programme, beginning with the traditional parades, coronations and legend re-enactments. Around these elements of pageantry they add the races, competitions, and displays. These are the sanctioned events, organized by other groups who benefit from the marketing tie-in with the Carnival. Like a wedding there are things old and new, borrowed and freshly imagined, all subject to the whims of winter.

One Boreas, speaking of his costume, said, "People enjoy pageantry," and that has been an underlying feature of the Carnival. In the early Carnivals Borealis arrived as a King with his Queen. There do not seem to have been any coronations. In 1916 and 1917 the numerous queens received due honors at a ball, but with the Carnival revival of 1937 the Queen's Coronation became more of an event. Frank Madden (Boreas Rex III) wrote the book explaining the legend; Carl Gray (Boreas Rex V) saw to the grand outline; Bill Curtis often wrote the scripts; and Olivia Johnson, longtime committee chairman, made it all happen.

The minutes of 1937 meetings of the board of directors indicate that the coronation was first patterned after the Veiled Prophet's debutante "belle-of-the-ball" in St. Louis. Later the coronations of George VI in London in 1939, and of his daughter Elizabeth II in 1952, would be the sources. St. Paul's Westminster Abbey would be the Auditorium. Sets built by Gordon Shumaker transformed it into the throne room, or Great Hall of Jupiter. Entertainment featured some of the marching bands with their majorettes, as well as local orchestras, the Andahazy Ballet Borealis, and choirs. In the early years Boreas Rex received his crown before the first weekend, and his Queen was crowned on the following Tuesday. After 1984 the king's and queen's events merged. Senior and Junior royalty have separate coronations.

Those who planned or saw the Queen's Coronations from the late 1930s through the 1950s recall them as extraordinary occasions, must-see events, or, as Helen Duffy Murphy said, "It was just IT in those days." Olivia Johnson is given much of the credit for the development of the event. She was a personal shopper at Field-Schlick's, well acquainted with St. Paul society, and a stickler for details. The Coronations which she planned as chairman, said Lorraine Venaas, who worked with her, were well-rehearsed and on time. She was not afraid to chastise even a visiting star such as Jimmy Dean when he came late to a Coronation rehearsal. In 1966 the Coronation was dedicated to Olivia Johnson. She had helped to stage twenty-five of the pageants, serving for eighteen years as the chairman.

Coronations took place in the Auditorium. First the visiting princesses and out-of-town royalty entered. Then the queen candidates and their escorts made their way into the Auditorium, where they would stand in line, facing each

Program for the 1987 royal coronation.

other. Down the center of the double row walked the Lord High Chamberlain, followed by pages carrying the queen's mantle. The Chamberlain walked slowly, paused in front of one girl, walked a little further, paused again, until finally reaching the princess who would be queen. She received the armful of red roses and would don the queen's mantle, as she went to receive the tiara from her King. From 1939 until 1957 Herb Schell took the role of Lord High Chamberlain and, by all accounts, heightened the drama of the Coronation much as Bert Parks once did for the Miss America pageant. Schell became Boreas Rex XXIII in 1959.

Coronations take place at the beginning of the Carnival, while the storming of the Ice Palace by Vulcanus and his Krewe marks the ritual ending. Winter, so it seems, is over; Boreas and Aurora will depart for the North, while Spring and Summer, thanks to the Fire King, are now on their way.

In the first Carnivals those who attacked were each provided with interesting ammunition: Roman candles and large firecrackers. Charles Ingles, a St. Paul librarian, marched with the High School Toboggan Club in 1886 and thought the storming was grand, although he couldn't really see it from his spot in the procession. Ingles wrote in his journal:

... on every hand were the Roman candles, while high on the central tower of the castle burst large bombs which scattered red, blue, green and purple lights. The interior of the palace was lighted up with red fire and the palace was surrounded by thousands of uniformed club members carrying torches...After the siege had lasted some time a truce was declared and the two kings joined forces, the Ice King riding in the Fire King's chariot. We

escorted the kings around the city… The whole line of march was illuminated with red and blue lights, fire works were sent off in profusion and in the business blocks the windows were illuminated by hundreds of candles. (Charles J. Ingles, *Journals*, 1884-1897, Vol. 1, p. 180, MHS).

That was the way a storming of the Ice Palace was supposed to proceed, with throngs of people in Carnival costumes and fireworks brilliantly lighting the night sky. In 1896 warm weather kept the builders from finishing the walls to their full, projected height. On the night of the storming it rained. A cartoon in the *St. Paul Dispatch* showed a very sad looking attacker, carrying his snowshoes as he left the Palace in the downpour, unable to complete his task.

Fireworks meant not only the Roman candles carried by Charles Ingles and his fellow marchers, but all sorts of "bombs bursting in air" and displays. One arrangement involved wires stretched to the ice palace from distant parts of the grounds. According to one reporter:

At the farthest point a bomb will be attached to the wire. It will go buzzing along following the wire and emitting a shower of sparks until it strikes the castle wall when it will explode with a report like a cannon (St. Paul Daily Globe, February 8, 1886).

Either preceding the storming of the palace or following it would come set displays of fireworks by the Pain Company of St. Paul. Floating stars, jeweled palms, fiery monkeys, Chinese war balloons, a trail of fire like one shown at the Chicago World's Fair, and finally, "The Falls of Niagara" were all part of the fireworks show at the 1896 Carnival.

For most Carnivals, parades, coronations and

the final assault comprised the ritual program. In 1916 and 1917 Louis W. Hill felt a pageant was needed. There were contests in each of these years for a pageant script and the final productions were among the events filmed by visiting movie cameramen. Tableaux vivants, masquerades, and costumed parties had long been part of St. Paul social life. The great age of the historical pageant certainly found expression in Minnesota with many communities celebrating their history in the scenes of a pageant, using hundreds of local actors. Such historical efforts were produced in St. Paul in 1911 and 1914, as prelude to the revived Carnival.

The second of the Midway Carnivals had an Indian pageant at the Hippodrome as part of the Coronation event. Later Carnival committees omitted separate pageants, since skating shows, rodeos, majorette performances and television programs filled the weeks of Carnival.

The Midway pageant with its Indian theme in 1929 referred back to Indian participation in the first Carnivals. Next to the 1886 Ice Palace stood the tepees of the Sioux village, whose residents had been invited by St. Paul's oldest inhabitant, A. L. Larpenteur; the invitation extended was both appropriate and perverse. Appropriate because no one could demonstrate better how to live and enjoy winter in Minnesota than its Indian inhabitants, but perverse since most Sioux no longer lived in the state as a result of the Sioux Uprising. Had this Carnival been held twenty years earlier, perhaps just after statehood in 1858, visitors could have toured an actual Indian village, Little Crow's Kaposia, just south of St. Paul. Had the visitors come with author Fredrika Bremer in 1850 they would have noticed that, as she wrote, "the city thronged with Indians." But after the events of the late

> "There is nothing that so heartens a city as a play time. There is nothing that kills it so dead as a constant veneer of assumed dignity. A city that cannot play and laugh and shout and have fun with itself is unforgivably stupid."
>
> ~ Duluth News Tribune (July 3, 1916).

summer of 1862 in New Ulm, most Sioux families had been forced to leave the state. Thus, the seventy-five Sioux people who came to the Carnival journeyed from their homes in North Dakota territory.

The tepees they used were set on wooden floors with holes cut in the center for fires. It was hoped that the Sioux would show Carnival visitors aspects of daily life such as cooking, singing, and dancing. One year the dancing included a war dance after which the Sioux were invited to share a peace pipe with visiting Ojibwe. Indian men entered snowshoe and foot races, and guided their dogs, horses, moose and elk in sled and travois parades. Indian women told stories and made moccasins which found a ready market among the members of the marching clubs.

Sioux families came to the three 1880s Carnivals as well as to the 1896 event. That year one reporter learned that two of the older men present had been among those arrested in 1862. They were reprieved by President Lincoln, then sent to Rock Island, Illinois, and finally to Fort Totten, near Devil's Lake, North Dakota. Justice Flandrau, Borealis IV, had directed the defense of New Ulm in 1862 but his thoughts concerning the Sioux in the Carnival village were not recorded and the Indians did not respond to the reporters (*The Daily Pioneer Press*, January 24, 1896).

In 1916 there were both tepees and Indians present, but the tepees were used as warming houses for skaters or tobogganers. The ten tepees were placed by the Cedar Street, Ramsey Hill and Harriet Island rinks or slides. The Indians were Blackfeet tribal members who came from Louis Hill's Glacier Park. Charles M. Flandrau wrote appreciatively of the tepees. He thought nothing could be

> more interesting, more decorative, more appropriate than these primitive habitations with their genial fires in the center. They were Minnesota, they belonged to us and our landscape, they had become tradition, but they were really history (St. Paul Pioneer Press, February 6, 1916).

In 1917 the tepee poles stood along the Ice Palace walls, holding flags, while other tepees sheltered the sled dog racers and their animals. While an Indian-themed Carnival would take place in 1929, the Indian village was gone for good.

In 2003 a pow-wow was held in Landmark Center featuring Indian dancing, costumes, and food. Georgia Lickness, a member of the Leech Lake Band of Ojibwe, organized the event which she said pointed to the long history of Indian involvement with the Carnival (St. Paul Pioneer Press, January 19, 2003, B1).

Starry Nights In St. Paul

Inviting special guests to the Winter Carnival has long been the custom. Political leaders, military men, Arctic explorers, and entertainers have all been on Carnival committees' lists.

Some merely appear and ride in the parades, often designated as "Grand Marshals." Others, especially in the Geisler years, came to entertain.

The honored guests themselves were entertained at the dinners and balls of Carnival weeks, and were expected to ride in the Grande Day and Torchlight parades aboard the most elegant of

floats. In 1886 Lieutenant Adolphus Washington Greely, the Arctic explorer, was invited, but declined and arranged instead for a display of objects from his recent explorations to be sent. Continuing the polar explorers theme in 1887, Lieutenant Frederic Schwatka who had recently been in Yellowstone National Park, was supposed to arrive with his dog and moose trains to inspect the Ice Palace. Unfortunately, a blizzard which brought welcome snow to Minnesota also kept Lieutenant Schwatka in Montana.

Many years later another polar explorer sent a gift to the Carnival. Admiral Richard E. Byrd brought back penguins from his second expedition to the South Pole. John F. Scott (Boreas Rex VII in 1941) decided St. Paul should have penguins in the parades. After a request made to Admiral Byrd, Polar Pete and Antarctic Annie rode on the Minnesota Federal float and afterwards took up residence at the Como Park Zoo. For those who know the classics of children's literature it would be the second time a polar

Senator Rudy Boschwitz walking in the 1990 Torchlight Parade.

explorer had sent penguins to Minnesota. In Richard and Florence Atwater's charming story of a Stillwater housepainter, *Mr. Popper's Penguins* (1938), it is "Admiral Drake" who telephones to say that a certain gift is on the way north, beginning Mr. Popper's new life.

George Esslinger, originally from South St. Paul, brought his huskies to Victory Square for the Carnival in 1946. The dogs were a part of the Army Air Force's Arctic Search and Rescue unit. When snow made evacuating the wounded from the Battle of the Bulge in World War II more difficult, Esslinger and his dogs managed to save many of them. For those who recalled the Winnipeg-to-St. Paul dogsled race of 1917, seeing these huskies camping downtown and

Visitors at the 1917 parade, including Governor J. A. A. Burnquist, the "March King" John Philip Sousa, and Boreas II, J. P. Elmer.

riding on the Emporium department store's float, must have been startling.

Joining Boreas and the Queen of the Snows on two occasions were famous Minnesotans who had actually traveled to the Arctic. Ann Bancroft of St. Paul, the first woman to reach the North Pole on foot, was asked to be the Grand Marshal of the 1987 parade. Ten years later Paul Schurke of Ely who had been part of the same expedition served as parade Grand Marshal.

Louis Hill's guest lists were probably the largest for any Carnival as they included his business colleagues, royalty of other civic festivals and political leaders. The most frequently shown image of the 1917 Carnival is one of Boreas Rex II, Minnesota Governor J. A. A. Burnquist, Carnival queens, and John Philip Sousa, all standing on the steps of the State capitol. Sousa wasn't technically speaking a special guest. He was already appearing at the Auditorium with his band as a part of a musical ice show called "Hip Hip Hooray." The skating star was Charlotte Oelschlagel, a German figure skater. The show had been booked into St. Paul previously and would leave before the actual opening of the Carnival, so a special parade of the marching clubs on January fifteenth was arranged.

Among Hill's guests were King Pip of the Spokane Apple Festival and Ring Lardner who accompanied a group of Spanish athletes to St. Paul from Chicago. Lardner, then writing for the *Chicago Tribune*, went home before the end of the dogsled race and wrote a quite bemused column on the subject. He evidently was not enamored of the cold, the dogsled race, or the dogs.

For the 1937 Carnival another bandleader appeared. Rudy Vallee and his Connecticut Yankees not only performed during Carnival week in St. Paul, but could be heard on the 125 radio stations of NBC's red network. This, obviously, was the ideal situation for the Carnival as national publicity came from their star guest and from those who appeared on his show. That year CBS broadcast the king's coronation and NBC's blue network stations told the country about the Grande day parade. *The St. Paul Dispatch* and the Minnesota Amusement Company underwrote the appearance of Rudy Vallee and his Connecticut Yankees.

The radio broadcasts of the pre-war Carnivals and newsreel coverage of the parades and sporting events were important to the success of these years, when Martin Kelly served as managing director. It was his idea, evidently, to have the parade pass through the Auditorium, creating not only a more comfortable venue for the audience, but a revenue source for the Carnival.

Not all guests could or would entertain. Five young ladies from Canada came in 1952 who were not celebrities of that sort. The Dionne Quintuplets (Annette, Cecile, Emilie, Marie and Yvonne) had become famous simply by being born, in 1934. As babies and young children the Quints had been featured in movies, advertising and as dolls and toys. Their images had sold calendars in the millions, first in a calendar painting by Gil Elvgren for the Louis F. Dow firm of St. Paul, and then in calendar photographs for Brown & Bigelow. It was Charles Ward, that firm's president, who brought the Quints to St. Paul. They rode on the calendar company's float, wearing white capes, and seated behind leaping white reindeer. Float-maker Bob Edgett recalls that when the float came up the ramp into the St. Paul Auditorium the reindeer seemed ready to rise up and fly away. The Brown & Bigelow float with the Dionnes on board won the Sweepstakes Award that year when the theme was "Call of the North."

The Dionne Quintuplets are riding on a float in the 1952 parade.

Just as radio and the newsreels shown in the movie theaters represented publicity during the late 1930s and 1940s, the "television years" best described the period from 1952 to 1970 when John Geisler served as managing director for the Winter Carnival. His predecessor, Walter Van Camp, had left to head the Seattle Seafair organization. Geisler was recruited from the Aberdeen, South Dakota, Snowfest, which perhaps explains why so many Winter Carnival royalty have visited that pageant.

John Geisler was able to convince both individual television stars and variety shows to come to St. Paul. Local sponsors helped. Whirlpool sponsored the broadcast of the seventy-fifth anniversary parade on NBC, and Hamm's brought Mitch Miller and his show in 1963. The stars and their shows began with Ed Sullivan's "Toast of the Town" in 1954. The appropriately titled game show named "Queen for a Day" came in 1958. Garry Moore (1961) and Steve Allen (1963) followed. "Strike it Rich" (1956) and "Let's Make a Deal" (1967) also broadcast from St. Paul during Carnival week. Stars who appeared included Eddie Fisher (1954), Dinah Shore (1957), Pat Boone (1960), Forrest Tucker (1972), and Carmel Quinn (1975). John Geisler left the Winter Carnival in 1970 for a job at the Hamm's Brewery, as director of public relations. After his departure the era of the big shows and big stars slowly came to an end.

For some the television stars brought the excitement and national publicity that the Carnival lacked. Even earlier, in the letter of resignation which Martin Kelly wrote to the Carnival board of directors, he suggested that St. Paul businesses expected that sort of national spotlight, in return for their Carnival support. Kelly wrote:

> I contend that the national acceptance of this Carnival has been the one most important step in selling it to our St. Paul people.... And I contend that when the national buildup starts to fade the end of the Saint Paul Winter Carnival is in sight (Letter of May 6, 1940, SPWCA Papers, MHS.)

Kelly stated that his connection with the Minnesota Amusement Company (the theatrical chain that had grown out of the Finkelstein–Ruben partnership) had made such promotion and publicity possible and that was what St. Paul businesses wanted. Kelly suggested that the Carnival needed someone with the theater links he had. Kelly was perhaps unaware that L. N. Scott had previously provided those connections for the 1916 and 1917 Carnivals.

For others the focus on imported entertainment and indoor activities was a mistake and an abandonment of the Carnival's primary goal of promoting St. Paul. It is certainly true that televising a parade affects its duration by limiting the amount of coverage as well as its audience, since many might then prefer to watch it at home. The publicity that came because of the stars and their broadcasts was welcome, yet Carnival committees would always have to decide whether it helped or hindered their mission.

On The Ice, On Your Mark, Go!

"Could you do it on ice, or on snow? Could it be a race, or a contest, or a demonstration?" While these might sound like proper queries to pose in planning a Winter Olympics, they apply equally to the Winter Carnival. The Carnival has been a sports festival since its first year.

Some of the sports offered were familiar ones in St. Paul. Curling, for example, was well known as a Scottish pursuit. Horse racing on ice and ice skating were familiar, but tobogganing, snowshoeing, and anything done on skis were new concepts. Inviting the outside world to see Minnesotans enjoying themselves trying all of these icy pastimes involved a learning curve for both visitor and resident. "Flood the rink, build the slide, and they will come" meant "and they will learn" as well.

Toboggans, wrote J. H. Hanson in *The Crystal Carnival*, had been unknown in the United States before being featured at the Montreal Carnivals. Now, he thought, people preferred them to sleds for comfort, speed, and the softer landing after a spill.

Humorist Bill Nye wrote that the close quarters on a toboggan could be uncomfortable, especially if the heavy lady behind you was sticking her wet moccasins (and her equally soaked feet) into your overcoat pockets. Still, he commented gamely, he did want to take a trip on a toboggan. He was going to slide down that toboggan flume if he perished in the attempt. After all, he wrote, "A man who had ridden a cyclone, slid down a mountain in a gold-pan and been married nine years ought not to be afraid of a toboggan" (*St. Paul Daily Globe*, February 8, 1886).

Most people did not share Nye's trepidation. There were toboggan slides built for the children and adults at the 1886 Carnival, shared by forty-seven toboggan clubs with 2,800 members. Club members, like Charles Ingles, found the toboggan runs were "splendid sport" even at night, in minus thirty degree weather. Toboggan or sled

runs have been built for every Carnival since 1886. Usually one or more is in the proximity of an Ice Palace, often within its outer walls, but chutes have been placed on the Capitol Mall, on Dayton's Bluff, and down Ramsey Hill, among other hilly venues. Tobogganing was a sport available to anyone provided with the price of admission, the Carnival badge.

Snowshoeing was even more available to all comers. All that was needed was a snowy place to hike. Snowshoes, wrote Mr. Hanson, were of Canadian Indian origin and came in different sizes, depending on whether the wearer was a club member, surveyor, or lumberman. Moccasins were the correct footwear to use with snowshoes and the correct outfit to wear was the blanket uniform with its toque.

The St. George's Snow-Shoe Club, a Canadian group which hoped to open branches in American cities, established the rules for the

In the Wake of the News by Ring W. Lardner

Riverside, Feb. 1.

Friend Harvey: - Well Harvey here I am back in Riverside and I had to come back before the finish of the dog race because I couldn't stand the tropical climate of St. Paul. I would like to of seen the dogs and especially their drivers because I have always been interested in the various forms of insanity and if you think the drivers in this dog race are all there, listen to what they have to do.

In the first place they got to live with their dogs from the time dogs are puppys so as the dogs will get use to them and not bite out a couple of your vitals every time you get close enough. And then when the dogs are old enough to race you got to train them to keep going because their natural ambition is something like mine, to lay down and rest every chance they get. And you got to train them to go without food or water for a whole day at a time and live on nothing only the snow they can lap up when they ain't too busy mushing, which is dog-race for mooching along.

After you get them in shape, then you look at a sporting calendar and find out how many races you can enter this year and the schedule calls for one big race which is 522 miles from Winnipeg to St. Paul. The prize for the winner is $500 and I can't think of no easier way to earn $500 unless it would be to jump off the roof of THE TRIBUNE building on a bet. Because the driver isn't supposed to ride no more of the way than he has to on acct. of his weight making it harder for the dogs to pull the sled. And he's got to do most of his sleeping in snowdrifts and live on icicles and whatever frozen fish the dogs leave over at the fish stations.

Well Harvey you can tell how much they leave over by the friction that come off between two dogs on Mr. Hartman's team on acct. of one of the two

being ravenous. They wasn't no fish station in sight, so what does this dog do but pretend his own team mate is fish and eat him while he wasn't looking.

Theys five dogs to a team and no substitutes setting along the bench, so when one of Mr. Hartman's dogs eat the other, Mr. Hartman had to mush along with four and that meant he couldn't ride a step of the way because four dogs can't stand the pull. So he's been running ever since the 4th of July or whenever they started and the last thing we heard before we come away was that the dog that had eat the other was so sick of his bargain that he had to quit too and now they were carrying him on the sled till he gets better and Mr. Hartman's mushing behind three dogs.

The racing dogs are nice and clubby with outsiders too and the minute a man that isn't their master goes close enough to them they relieve him of one or two arms and legs for a practical joke.

Well some people asked me would I get on a special train with them and ride up to the North Dakota boundary and look at the dog teams and encourage them with applause. So I asked if it was any colder there than St. Paul and they says only 40 or 50 degrees but you didn't feel it. And then I asked if the dogs was safe to go near them and they says they wouldn't bite nobody they couldn't reach.

So here I am Harvey and I'm glad to see most of the snow melted off because Mr. Hartman keeps getting lost all the time on acct. of having to pay attention to one sick dog while he talks universal peace to the three others. And his team might accidentally mush into Riverside some morning and take us for fish.

Respy, R.

~ Chicago Tribune *(February 1, 1917).*

Curling was an important sport at the 1917 Carnival. Courtesy of the Minnesota Historical Society.

Children wait eagerly for dogsled rides in the park in this early photograph.

ered of Indian origin men from the Indian villages were asked to compete in races, even in something called a steeplechase event.

While there were six skating clubs with 400 members the emphasis was placed on races of various lengths with prizes awarded. By 1896 the speedskating field already included its share of stars who expected to be paid appearance fees. The stars did not show up because, it was reported, their demands "had been ignored with silent contempt, and the races will be better off for their absence" (*St. Paul Pioneer Press,* January 24, 1896). In other words, local amateur skaters had their chance.

Skating and curling rinks were usually arranged near the Ice Palaces where the ice conditions could be monitored. The curling teams or rinks in the 1886 competition came from both Canadian and American cities, but it was a Minneapolis team which won the competition, or bonspiel. The winners took home a gold bar and pin with a pendant shield engraved with crossed brooms. That club had been organized in 1884 by an immigrant from Scotland named Hastings. He was a stonecutter by trade who made his own curling stones (*St. Paul Daily Globe,* February 14, 1886).

Other competitive events in the early Carnivals included horse racing (the course was along Summit Avenue), a long-jump for skaters, and what was identified as polo although an illustration showed men wielding curved sticks on ice, but with no horses.

Louis Hill's Carnivals were described and identified as Outdoor Sports festivals. A new century and a new organization meant that additional events appeared on the schedules. Tug-o-war, for example, and pushball were new. Ice tennis and ice baseball were offered, as were

clubs. When club members went out as a group, they were on a "tramp," led by a captain, and kept in line by his "whipper-in." At the end of a tramp the snowshoers adjourned to a club or a hotel where a light lunch was served. Pipes were smoked, but dissipation was not countenanced. Then the Club members sang songs and called out the Club yell as they performed a snake dance. Hanson's words suggest that men were the only snowshoe club members, but women did join. Since snowshoeing was consid-

The 1917 queen candidate of the Minnehaha Dry Cleaning Company Marching Club poses with a pushball at the Town and Country Club golf course.

The toboggan slide for the 1917 Carnival was located near the State Capitol.

An early version of a snowmobile was driven at the 1916 Carnival by members of the Northern Pacific Railroad Marching Club.

Ski-joring at the 1917 Carnival at the Town and Country Club golf course.

snowshoe races, curling, hockey, ski-joring (which featured skiers being pulled by horses), and motorsled races. Motorsled races were held at the State Fairgrounds and on Lake Phalen. The motorsled was, as it sounds, an engine mounted on skis. Add a propeller behind the driver's seat and it became an aerosled. There were about twelve of these prototype snowmobiles available to race in St. Paul. Their day was yet to come.

Ten toboggan slides were built in various neighborhoods of the city. Ski jumping was available on Harriet Island. Skating rinks were there and in Rice Park, near the Queen's palace. Skaters could see Charlotte demonstrate her skills on the "Hip Hip Hooray" rink, named after the musical show then being staged in St. Paul.

Between parades, pageants, newsreel filming, and sporting events, the Hill Carnival days were crowded. The most famous sporting event of 1917, however, turned out to be the dogsled race. It was Louis Hill's idea to recreate a trip made by his father, James J. Hill, from Winnipeg to St. Paul. The "Red River Derby" followed what was known as the Pembina Trail for oxcarts and the tracks of the Great Northern railway. The 522 mile route led from Winnipeg south along the Red River of the north to Grand Forks, crossing into Minnesota after reaching Fargo, then continuing to Fergus Falls, Alexandria, and St. Cloud, before winding up in St. Paul's Como Park.

This race was described as a "go-as-you-please" with each driver and his team of five dogs stopping to eat and rest as they needed. Frozen fish were shipped by rail to feed the dogs; the drivers dined en route on fried fish, bread, and tea which they brewed in the kettle each carried. Townspeople along the way offered food and lodging. The contestants in the race were Cree mixed bloods from Manitoba, other men of Icelandic descent from Canada, and two Americans. Their dogs were collies, huskies related to some used by Ernest Shackleton in the Antarctic, and other wolfhound, St. Bernard, and husky crossbreeds. Merrill Jarchow wrote in *Minnesota History* that commentary at the time contrasted both the skills and ethnicity of the dogs and their drivers.

In the end it was one of the Americans, Fred Hartman, who came in last, but was the star of the show. His dogs fought, leading to the death of his lead dog. Later another dog became lame so Hartman not only had to lead his team on foot, but traveled with four rather than the five dogs which other teams drove. The race lasted from January twenty-fourth until February third, with an exhausted Hartman arriving in Como Park four hours after the other drivers. The next evening dogs and drivers appeared at a show in the Auditorium. This was followed by a week of appearances at the Strand Theatre and a benefit performance at the State Fairgrounds.

Another type of race, certainly shorter and less arduous than the dogsled affair of 1917, was planned for the Midway Carnival of 1930. That year the Ice Palace built at Dunning field was the focal point of activities so that was the terminus of a cross country ski race. Skiers began at the Fort Snelling Round Tower, followed West Seventh street to Edgcumbe Road (then newly opened) and then continued the rest of the six mile route to the Ice Palace. The race was held at night with mounted police and illumination to keep skiers from losing their way. The idea behind the race was to demonstrate the use of skis as transportation, according to C. A. Lund, president of Northland Ski Company, who chaired the committee (*St. Paul Dispatch*, January 29, 1930).

Bill Grayson and his team were participants in the 1917 race from Winnipeg to St. Paul. Courtesy of the Minnesota Historical Society.

Fred Hartman, 1917 dogsled racer, is shown with his lead dog in Rice Park. Courtesy of the J. J. Hill Library.

Eight years later skiers entering the Arrowhead Ski Derby completed a five-day trek of 153 miles from Duluth to St. Paul. And in 1956 U. S. Army ski troopers, based in Colorado, came to Minnesota to ski from Pine City to the Keller golf course in St. Paul. Then they were taken by helicopter to the State Capitol where they delivered a flaming torch to open the Carnival's programs (*White Bear Press*, January 28, 1956). Lund's concept of cross country skis as transportation for the military or for pleasure had certainly been proven.

Some sporting events were unique, one-time only, such as the Red River Derby of 1917, the trials for the U. S. Olympic speedskating team in 1947, or the American Bowling Congress National championships in 1941. Other races and competitions were held every year, for years, sometimes even if a Carnival did not take place. The *St. Paul Daily News* sponsored what were called Mutt Races, beginning in 1917 at the State Fairgrounds oval. Children on sleds, pulled by family pets, competed. Mutt races were held every year, whether there was a Carnival or not, although the newspaper's demise in the 1930s meant a change in sponsorship.

A Scandinavian ski club was organized in St. Paul in the fall of 1885, becoming one of the earliest, if not the first, to be founded in the United States. This was at a time when many Americans weren't sure whether to pronounce "ski" as "she" or "sky," and whether the actual equipment was an emaciated toboggan or a webless snowshoe. Illustrations of the club members in action show them flying simultaneously down one of the ski jump hills, each clutching his single pole with both hands, sweeping it from side to side to balance himself. A two-pole ski technique would be introduced later on.

Skiers used the toboggan runs during the first Carnival, creating jumps by placing heaps of snow at the end of the slides. The next year an actual contest was scheduled, for the renamed Ski and Kjelke Club. Kjelkes were a form of toboggan, seven feet long and two feet high, with runners. When the club marched members carried their skis and pulled the kjelkes.

In 1916 and 1917 skiers could use actual ski jumps on steel scaffolds built on Harriet Island (in 1916) and at West Seventh Street and Alaska Avenue (in 1917). Nearly 15,000 people watched the National Ski Jumping Tournament on January 20 and 30, 1917, with the first day for amateur competitions, and the second for the professionals.

When the Winter Carnival began activities once again in 1937 the St. Paul Ski Club organized tournaments at its Mound Park slide until it blew down and a new facility was built. The Battle Creek 60-meter slide was used for competition from 1939 until 1974. The Battle Creek slide was built by WPA workers and was probably designed by Ice Palace architect Cap Wigington. Ski Club historians Tom Harrington and Wally Wakefield note in their book on the St. Paul Ski Club that when the Battle Creek slide was dismantled the scaffold steel was purchased by a ski club in Ely, Minnesota.

Harriet Island was one of two sites for the 1916 Outdoor Sports Carnival. Planned for this location were a ski jump, toboggan slide, and one of the two Ice Palaces. Lithograph from Official Souvenier (sic) Program (1916). Courtesy of Bob Jackson.

Ice fishing contest at White Bear Lake during the 1948 Carnival. Courtesy of the Minnesota Historical Society.

Aerial view of the 1950 White Bear Lake ice fishing contest. Each year a different pattern was used to separate fishing areas from unplowed lake ice. Courtesy of the Minnesota Historical Society.

Winter Carnival ski jumping tournament director in 1939 was Louis W. Hill, Jr., a lifetime member of the St. Paul Ski Club. Hill's interest in skiing extended to scheduling races on the family's North Oaks property (a street named Ski Lane along the North Oaks golf course commemorates these races). For many years a rope tow aided skiers to ascend a small hill in North Oaks, known to residents as "Mr. Hill's Hill."

White Bear Lake has a long history of involvement in Winter Carnival events. Its citizens sent sleighfuls of ice from the lake to help build the first Ice Palace. The lake itself has been the location for two long-running events: the World's Original Ice Fishing Contest and, occasionally, for the Hot Air Balloon races that started in 1962.

For many years the World's Original Ice Fishing Contest was one of the Winter Carnival's most popular events. The first year (1947) sponsors expected perhaps two hundred fishermen to enter; but 605 showed up. The contest was co-sponsored by the White Bear Rod and Gun Club and the *St. Paul Pioneer Press and Dispatch*. Nearly four-dozen prizes were offered for the largest fish, the heaviest fish, the first angler to land a fish, and the fisherman who caught the most fish. Fishermen had to dig, drill, or chop their own holes in the ice, and were limited to one line and one hook. Bass were to be caught, measured, and released, and perch were ignored. James La Boie of White Bear Lake caught the largest fish, a six pound, two ounce Northern in that first tournament (*White Bear Press*, January 31, 1947).

By 1952 fishermen needed to purchase a Winter Carnival button or an ice fishing button to enter the contest and 5,200 people did so. Ed Sanders who caught a five pound three and three-quarters ounce northern pike won a trophy, a fishing boat, and a Martin 4½ horsepower motor for his efforts. For the first contest organizers had simply shoveled a long rectangular area for the fishermen. Later on, high school students from White Bear Lake entered a contest to design the fishing area. In 1952 the winning design was a 4-H clover to honor that organization's fiftieth anniversary. The 1956 design honored the March of Dimes with crossed crutches inside a large circle. Newspaper and magazine photographers seemed to like the aerial shots of fishermen scattered inside the carefully designed contest area.

The 1956 fishing derby attracted 7,500 entrants and was won by Gerald Picha who hooked a five pound, fifteen ounce walleye. Through the 1960s and 1970s the Ice Fishing contests retained their popularity. Several thou-

sand persons entered each year with entry fees now rising to $30.00 or more, and winners taking home prizes such as snowmobiles. But in the 1980s there was competition. Forest Lake sponsored a fishing contest and there were similar events on nearby lakes. The World's Original Fishing Contest was no more.

Hot air balloons rising from the ice of White Bear Lake to float gently away in the winter sky provide one of the loveliest Carnival images. The sport of hot air balloon racing was introduced to Minnesota and Carnival history by Don Piccard. He actually landed his first solo flight in the White Bear area. Piccard took off from Parade Stadium in Minneapolis in a Japanese mulberry paper balloon, captured during World War II, and landed on the Arcand brothers' farm three miles northeast of town (*White Bear Press*, February 21, 1947). Fifteen years later Piccard would organize the first Winter Carnival balloon event, in 1962, perhaps the country's first competitive race for hot air balloons.

Piccard arranged for sponsors, the link with the Winter Carnival, and obtained a Revere sterling silver bowl as the trophy. Three balloonists flew: Ed Yost, Dick Keuser, and Tracy Barnes. It was Barnes who won that first race, flying in a home-made balloon fashioned from parachutes. Barnes was sponsored by the Red Owl grocery stores. Piccard named the prize for his balloonist father, the Jean Piccard Trophy for Thermal Balloons. This prize was offered for the last time in 1971, when it was won by Bert and Judy Bigelow.

Races then were not about speed or distance, but accuracy, in what was called "hare and hound" races. One balloon, designated as the hare, goes up. After a flight of 45 to 60 minutes, the pilot selects a landing site and lands. He then takes two pieces of fabric, fifty feet long, and creates an "X". Pilots of the hound balloons try to land as close as possible to the "X". The winner of this contest, in 1985, received $1,500.00.

Matt Wiederkehr saw that first balloon race in 1962 and immediately determined to fly a hot air balloon himself. He contacted the balloon maker, Raven Industries of Sioux Falls, South Dakota, and within a few years had realized that dream. Weiderkehr, a development engineer at 3M, founded the Minnesota Aerostat Society at work. He and his wife Bobbie took on the task of managing the Hot Air Balloon races for the next twenty-three years. Needed each year were funds to cover the balloonists' costs for lodging, propane, and insurance, and for the trophies and prizes. Balloon races were started from White Bear Lake and other venues.

In 1983 a group of aviation enthusiasts organized the United States Air and Space Bicentennial to celebrate 200 years of flight in America. One event was to be selected to represent each aspect of aviation. When Matt Wiederkehr heard of the program he immediately determined to have the Winter Carnival race represent hot air ballooning. At first the launch of the space shuttle Challenger was to kick off the Bicentennial celebration but the Challenger had a fuel leak and the launch had to be cancelled. The Bicentennial organizing committee then selected the balloons of St. Paul to begin their year. Any group that wanted to sponsor an event linked to the Air and Space Bicentennial was asked to contribute $1,000.00 to the United States Organizing Committee. George Albers of St. Paul, a local balloonist famed for the figure of the hunter "Orion" on his balloon, wrote that check and the Winter Carnival race became the first flying event of the Bicentennial. Balloons took off from the State Capitol grounds heading towards Cape Canaveral but landed four miles away in Woodbury. On the following day even more hot air balloons took off in a race from the State Fairgrounds.

Wiederkehr's balloon bore the official Bicentennial logo, but another balloon was equally official. Artist Dave Johnson painted the Norman Rockwell illustration, "Snow Sculpturing," onto a banner which was then attached with Velcro to the Brown & Bigelow balloon. The Rockwell artwork was used for the 1983 Winter Carnival button.

From the three balloon race of 1962 the Winter Carnival competitions drew interest, both locally and throughout the country. Festival directors from Indianola, Iowa (south of Des Moines), the Kentucky Derby, and the Albuquerque

In this 1972 race the hot air balloons left from St. Paul's downtown airport, Holman Field. Courtesy of Matt and Bobbie Wiederkehr.

Tenth Anniversary Hot Air Balloon Race . . . St. Paul Winter Carnival

Conducted by Matt Wiederkehr
Minnesota Balloon Advertising
1604 Euclid, St. Paul, Minn. 55106
(612) 774-5208

N2314

Hot Air Balloon competition all sought guidance from Matt and Bobbie Wiederkehr. These races, all of which continue today, can be said to be "children of the St. Paul Winter Carnival." For the Wiederkehrs, their own children, Donna and Denise, would also become successful as balloonists, setting numerous records while still teenagers in the family sport and occupation.

Skating, both fancy as early Carnivals described it, and speedskating, have been featured at every Carnival. Rinks were available for public skating and sometimes streets were flooded to create unusual skating locations. Fifth street between Wabasha and St. Peter became a Carnival skating rink in 1956 and 1978. In 1929 Washington street in front of the Elks Club became a rink. Alongside the ice, in a tent, George Rector of Rector's restaurant in New York City demonstrated recipes.

Skating shows made their appearance during Carnival week beginning with the fair Charlotte of 1917's "Hip Hip Hooray." In 1938 the Ice Palace was designed to serve as a stage set for an Olympic skater, Sweden's Vivi-anne Hulten. She appeared in a show called "Gay Blades" which also starred an Austrian skater named Karl Schaeffer. After touring with various ice shows, Miss Hulten returned to St. Paul in 1964. She opened a skating school in Maplewood where she taught generations of Minnesotans the skills of that sport. In 1939 nine-time American ladies' figure skating champion, Maribel Y. Vinson, produced the Winter Carnival Ice Revue. Ms. Vinson would later star in the "Ice Capades." This show was often sponsored by Saintpaulites, Inc. during Carnival seasons.

In the early Carnivals speedskating races took place on the Mississippi River as well as on area lakes. The National Outdoor Speedskating

Balloons being prepared for the 1983 flight from the Minnesota State Capitol grounds. Courtesy of Matt and Bobbie Wiederkehr.

Balloon race jacket patch from 1983. Courtesy of Matt and Bobbie Wiederkehr.

Championships were held on Lake Como between 1946 and 1982. When the Como rink was closed, speedskating took a breather. The opening of the $4.2 million John Rose Oval in Roseville in 1994 offered a new venue for a sport that had grown enormously in popularity.

It took almost fifty years before the strange little aerosleds and motorsleds of 1917 ventured onto Lakes Phalen or Como in their new incarnation as snowmobiles. The first events were short races of one-half mile in 1964 and 1965, but the following year a big-time international race was planned. The Hill dogsled race from

A 1941 speed skating race. Courtesy of the Minnesota Historical Society.

Skate sailing contest at the 1948 Carnival. Courtesy of the Minnesota Historical Society.

Winnipeg to St. Paul would be run again, with snowmobiles. It would be a four-day race stopping at Crookston, Fergus Falls and St. Cloud, with a $500 first prize.

Snowmobiles would follow where sled dogs led the way, but their Winnipeg-to-St. Paul route would be in ditches along roadways and 457 miles long. Temperatures never rose above fifteen below zero. One driver smashed his windshield when his vehicle hit a mailbox. Another driver, knowing that he had no chance of winning, went off the trail through a farm, hit a children's jungle gym, and then crashed into the side of a chicken coop. It took thirteen hours and thirty-six minutes for Herb Howe to reach St. Paul on his Polaris Colt and win the race. The following year, as defending champion, Howe collided with a parked car and demolished his machine.

Bill Vint, in his history of snowmobile racing, quotes another racer, Edson Brandt, on this particular problem faced by snowmobilers: parked cars. People watching a race often parked their cars close to dangerous spots or turns, wanting to observe how drivers handled them. Thus, additional obstacles were created for the racers. The 1967 race attracted 121 entrants, but had its fill of controversy. Racers accused other racers of illegal modifications to their machines and of cheating by trailering (placing their machines inside trucks for transport). Gerry Reese of Roseau, another Polaris driver, won the problem-plagued race.

Weather would always affect the Snowmobile races in the form of sub-zero temperatures, glaze ice conditions, and blizzards along the way. Machines broke down and accidents happened. Races were cut short due to fog (1973) and lack of snow (1968). In 1969 Hamm's decided to offer a prize to the racer who faced and overcame the most problems in the race, naming it the "True Grit" award. The 1971 True Grit winner, Erv Melvie of Viking, Minnesota, had to drive eighty miles on one ski, blew out three clutches, drove with a leaky fuel tank and no chaincase oil. But he was able to finish the race and claim his $1,000.00 award from the brewery.

Probably the peak year for what was now called the International 500 was in 1976 when 385 racers entered, and less than half finished the race. Rising gas prices affected the cost of the race and so, of course, did the weather. The 1976 race reversed the direction by heading north from St. Paul to Winnipeg. The direction was the same the following year, but weather ended that event at Thief River Falls. After other cancelled events the International 500 ended its competitions in 1982. In just under twenty years the Winter Carnival race had offered spectators an annual four days of racing excitement in these competitions, often using

Minnesota-built snowmobiles from Polaris and Arctic Cat pitted against the John Deere machines from Illinois. Prizes rose to $10,000.00 for the first place winner, making the triumph economically worthwhile. Although the International 500 is no longer held, shorter snowmobile races have been held on Lakes Como or Phalen. An oval track for snowmobile races was built in Como Park. The race there was called "Snowtona" with apologies to Daytona, Florida, another racing town.

The Winter Carnival's car racing on ice began in 1952, organized by members of the 3M Car Club and the Sports Car Club of America (SCCA). For the first five years races were held on a plowed mile and a half course on Lake Phalen. Cars entered cannot be longer than 190 inches and race on studded tires. Cars race on lakes frozen to a consistent depth of eighteen inches. The season lasts from January until early March; hence a race should usually be possible during the Winter Carnival. In recent years that race has been held on Forest Lake, at Thunder Bay, and in 2003, at

The 1981 Winnipeg to St. Paul snowmobile races. Courtesy of the Minnesota Historical Society.

The 1984 Marathon race was sponsored by Hamm's brewery.

Snoopy was the Grand Marshal of the 1990 Winter Carnival parade. He appeared on the official button, and also on kites given away for the Kite Festival.

Garrison on Mille Lacs lake. Today's races are organized by the Twin Cities chapter of the International Ice Racing Association.

Short foot races and sprints were held in the 1880s; longer races were added to Carnival programs after World War II. Because American runners had become interested in these longer distance events, the Winter Carnival added a marathon to its sports calendar in 1983. Sponsored by Hamm's, it was called "The Torturous 26 Marathon." Posters featured a pudgy Bear running with determination, but not speed, below the slogan "Get a Glimpse of the Ice Age!" The route began and ended at Holman Field, the downtown airport. Three years later, on a relatively balmy October weekend, the Twin Cities Marathon would be launched. The Winter Carnival races continued, but were more often at a Frozen 5K or Half Marathon distance.

The list of winter sports planned for Carnival season has grown enormously. There are the natural candidates which need ice or snow: skating, skiing, curling, hockey, ski-joring and games such as bandy and broomball. Then there are the warm weather events held in winter: golf on the snow, and slow pitch softball, both of which now have long Carnival histories. Horse racing, mutt races, car racing, kite flying and hot air balloon racing all attract crowds and participants, providing the answer to the question, "Can you play it on ice?" The answer is "Yes!"

Hunting For Treasure

Contests with prizes have always been part of Winter Carnival programming. Minnesotans of all ages have been invited to design posters, carve images of ice and snow, and write scripts for pageants. But of all the contests the most enthusiastically supported has probably been the Treasure Hunt. For serious treasure hunters, and there are many, guides to St. Paul parks and analyses of all previous Treasure Hunts exist, in print and on web sites.

The *St. Paul Pioneer Press* began the Treasure Hunt in 1952. Employees of the newspaper hid a small bronze medallion, at first in a treasure chest. A clue in rhyme was published each day in the paper's early edition suggesting the location of the medallion. Thirteen clues were written, but usually somebody found the hiding place before every clue appeared. From the very first year the Treasure Hunt attracted eager searchers who would spend hours wielding shovels in the city's parks and public spaces.

The medallion has been concealed in cookies, chunks of snow, a sink strainer, a White Castle hamburger box, and a tortilla chip can. It might be wrapped, stuffed, or stuck to something else.

For example, the eleventh clue in 1984 began:

*"They're made to be played
They're made to be broken."*

This clue led puzzle solvers, eventually, to the medallion's location on a broken 45 rpm record. "A symbol of luck" in 1967 meant that the medallion was attached to a horseshoe concealed near the Fairgrounds horse barn. Clues have noted distant landmarks and even slogans. "Name the brew that grew with the great Northwest" (in 1988) suggested Jacob Schmidt beer, the user of that tagline, and thus meant looking in Tony Schmidt Park in Arden Hills. That year the medallion was wrapped in almond bark candy.

The medallion is usually hidden in St. Paul, but on occasion treasure hunters have needed to search parks in suburban Ramsey County. Twice Maplewood's Wakefield Park was the spot (in 1971 and 1982), much to the distress of park administrators. One reporter described an army of hundreds of treasure hunters with "shovels of all kinds, hoes, rakes, picks, snow blowers, and, of course, metal detectors." In trying to locate the medallion trees were uprooted, bulbs dug from the gardens, and other damage done to park buildings, totaling almost $3,000.

Since 1988 the medallion, now bearing a design of the Ice Palace rather than the face of King Boreas, has been fabricated from plastic, eliminating the need for the metal detectors. Finding the medallion still takes many hours in often very cold weather, according to virtually every successful finder. The reward, of course, has grown. In 2001 the finder traded the medallion for a $10,000 prize, given by the *Pioneer Press* and by the St. Paul Festival and Heritage Foundation. Cathi Hogan, who had dug in many other Treasure Hunts, not only found the plastic disc in a Dove Soap box in Como Park, but she had saved the newspaper clues and registered her Winter Carnival Button with the Foundation, entitling her to the basic $2,500 prize plus $2,500 for the clipped clues, and a $5,000 bonus for the registered button.

A snow-less winter should mean easier hunting for the Medallion-seekers, but the clues in the 2003 Treasure Hunt proved very puzzling. Not until the last day and the last clue did the three winners discover the Medallion in a block of ice in Como Park, the city's only "park with a zoo" as clue number eleven read. Josh Stender, Craig Black, and Michael Corrigan won the prize plus a trip to Hawaii and $1,200 worth of groceries from Cub Foods (*St. Paul Pioneer Press*, January 31, 2003, B1).

Epilogue

By Robert Viking, President, St. Paul Festival and Heritage Foundation

Throughout history communities have celebrated. From the earliest of times when stone age tribes gathered to feast upon the spoils of the hunt, through the days when the returning Roman legions marched through the streets of Rome parading exotic treasures, to the present day when communities throughout the world celebrate their identity, humankind has celebrated.

Celebrations serve as unifying forces binding the historical, cultural, social and economic elements of the community. Celebrations build image, obtain favorable publicity, attract visitors, and serve as an economic stimulus. But most importantly, celebrations proclaim our identity as an ever-evolving community…Who we are, where we have come from, where we are going, and what we are striving for.

The Saint Paul Winter Carnival was created to counter the negative image of Minnesota's cold winters and to celebrate Saint Paul as the fastest growing city in the United States. The first Carnival was modeled after Mardi Gras and its tradition of feasting, dances and parades before a period of fasting. Similar to Mardi Gras there were masquerade balls and several parades, including one which has continued to this day,

the Torchlight Parade. Other activities included skiing, snowshoeing, ice skating, curling, tobogganing and horse racing on ice. Many of these activities have remained staples of today's Carnival while others such as horseracing on ice have evolved into activities such as dogsled races, snowmobile races, and car racing on ice. Similarly tobogganing has evolved into today's Giant Snow Slide. The first Carnival also gave birth to a Saint Paul icon, the Ice Palace. Fifteen super palaces have been built since 1886.

Today, the Saint Paul Winter Carnival continues to celebrate winter, build ice palaces, and proclaim the identity of our community. But the Carnival must meet several challenges if it is to continue to serve its function as a celebratory and unifying force in the community.

The Carnival must continue to evolve and reflect the changing cultural fabric of the community. Based upon the northern and western European traditions the Saint Paul Winter Carnival with its legend of Boreas Rex and Vulcanus Rex must be open to changes in its traditions if it is to embrace a community which today reflects an Asian, African, eastern European and Latino cultural tapestry.

The Carnival must meet the challenge of today's technological society with its increasing human isolation and serve as a unifying factor bringing people together for face-to-face human interaction. More than at any time in its history the Saint Paul Winter Carnival plays an essential role in bringing people together to communicate with one another and share their cultural heritage in an affordable, celebratory setting.

The relevance of all celebrations lies in their community ownership. Whether it be Mardi Gras, the Tournament of Roses, or the Saint Paul Winter Carnival, these, the oldest of the nation's celebrations, will survive only as long as their communities embrace them with a fierce loyalty.

Throughout the three centuries that the Saint Paul Winter Carnival has celebrated winter in Saint Paul, it has been confronted with many challenges – inhospitable weather, the Great Depression, two World Wars, social and technological revolution, and terrorism. The people of Saint Paul have come together and with their community celebration, the Saint Paul Winter Carnival, have met these challenges, played together in the snow, and have moved forward. There is no doubt that the spirited people of Saint Paul will meet current and future challenges and continue to celebrate their community.

Selected Bibliography

Books and Pamphlets

Fred Anderes and Ann Agranoff. *Ice Palaces.* New York, NY: Abbeville Press (1983).

S. T. Church. *Carnival Music and Song Folio.* St. Paul, MN: W. J. Dyer and Bro., Music Dealers (1887).

F. Scott Fitzgerald. "*The Ice Palace,*" in *Babylon Revisited and Other Stories.* New York, NY: Charles Scribner's Sons (1960): 1-24.

Rick Hamlin. *Tournament of Roses. A 100 Year Celebration.* New York, NY: McGraw Hill Book Company (1988).

J. H. Hanson. *An Idyl on Ice.* Illustrated by A. M. Doherty. St. Paul, MN: Chicago, St. Paul, Minneapolis & Omaha Railways (1887).

Tom Harrington with Wally Wakefield. On *Wings of Wood. A Summary of the First 100 years of the St. Paul Ski Club.* St. Paul, MN: The St. Paul Ski Club (1985).

Moira F. Harris. *The Paws of Refreshment. The History of Hamm's Beer Advertising.* St. Paul, MN: Pogo Press (1990).

General W.B. Hazen. *Our Barren Lauds,* Cincinnati, OH: Robert Clarke & Co., (1875).

Kirk and Lori Larson. *The Official 1987 Winter Carnival Treasure Hunters Guide.* St. Paul, MN (1987).

Paul Clifford Larson. *Icy Pleasures.* Afton, MN: Afton Historical Society Press (1998).

Robert Lavenda. *Corn Fests and Water Carnivals. Celebrating Community in Minnesota.* Washington, DC: Smithsonian Institution Press (1997): 81-92.

Frank Madden. *The Rollicking Realm of Boreas.* St. Paul, MN: Privately published (1941).

Karal Ann Marling. *Blue Ribbon. A Social and Pictorial History of the Minnesota State Fair.* St. Paul, MN: Minnesota Historical Society Press (1990).

Larry Millett. *Sherlock Holmes and the Ice Palace Murders.* New York, NY: Viking (1998).

Frank Moore. *Reminiscences of Pioneer Days in St. Paul.* St. Paul, MN: Pioneer Press Company (1908): 20, 21.

John Pfaender. *The First Hundred Years of the Town and Country Club*. St. Paul, MN: Town and Country Club (1988).

Bill Schwietz. *Ice Palaces & Buttons of the St. Paul Winter Carnival*. St. Paul, MN: Privately published (2002).

Colleen J. Sheehy, editor. *25 Years in the Heart of the Beast*. Minneapolis, MN: University of Minnesota Press (1999).

Thomas M. Spencer. *The St. Louis Veiled Prophet Celebration. Power on Parade, 1877-1995*. Columbia, MO: University of Missouri Press (2000).

David Vassar Taylor, with Paul Clifford Larson. Cap Wigington. *An Architectural Legacy in Ice & Snow*. St. Paul, MN: Minnesota Historical Society Press (2001).

Leroy F. Vaughn. *Vaughn's Parade and Float Guide*. Minneapolis, MN: T. S. Denison & Company (1956).

Bill Vint. *Warriors of Winter*. Milwaukee, WI: Market Communications, Inc. (1977).

Mary Lethert Wingerd. *Claiming the City: politics, faith and the power of place in St. Paul*. Ithaca, NY: Cornell University Press (2001).

_____ *St. Paul Centennial Ice Palace*. St. Paul, MN: Princeton Advertising (1986).

_____. *Winter Carnival 1990: A Report*. Directed by Robert H. Lavenda. St. Cloud, MN: St. Cloud State University Festival Research Project (1990).

_____ *St. Paul 1992 Super Palace*. St. Paul, MN: Superpalace Inc. (1992).

Periodicals

Fred Anderes and Ann Agranoff. "The Magic Chill of Ice Palaces still beckons us," *Smithsonian* 17:10 (January 1987): 62-69.

Don Boxmeyer. "Hot Stuff," *St. Paul Pioneer Press Dispatch* (January 26, 1990): C1, 2.

Don Boxmeyer. "The Lure and Lore of the Hunt," *St. Paul Pioneer Press Dispatch* (February 5, 1988): C1,2.

Don Boxmeyer. "Winter Carnival may not be gnome-less." *St. Paul Pioneer Press* (January 9, 2001).

Albert Britt. "St. Paul – the City that Discovered Winter," *Outing* LXIX: 6 (March 1917): 661-676.

Ralph Brown. "Fact and Fancy in Early Accounts of Minnesota's Climate," *Minnesota History* 17:3 (September 1936): 243-261.

James Taylor Dunn. "A Century of Song. Popular Music in Minnesota," *Minnesota History* 44:4 (Winter 1974): 122-135.

Karen McCoskey Goering. "Pageantry in St. Louis: History of the Veiled Prophet Organization," *Gateway Heritage* 4:4 (Spring 1984): 2-16.

Gareth Hiebert. "Asa, Gene, and their gnomes," *St. Paul Dispatch* (February 4, 1980): 11, 16.

Merrill E. Jarchow. "Hero: Frederick S. Hartman and the Winnipeg-to-St. Paul Dog Race," *Minnesota History* (Winter 1971): 283-294.

Mary Jean Jecklin. "Chilling tales. A history of the St. Paul Winter Carnival Ice Palaces," *Architecture Minnesota* (January/ February 1992): 20-23.

Ring Lardner. "In the Wake of the News," *Chicago Tribune* (February 2, 1917): 15.

Fred Lawshe. "Winter is for Fun. Brief History of Winter Sports Organizations," *Over the Years* IX:2 (April 1971): 2-3.

Jack Leonard. "Tailor to His Majesty Boreas," *St. Paul Pioneer Press*. Pioneer Magazine (January 27, 1952): 7-9.

John Francis Marion, "On New Year's Day in Philadelphia, Mummer's the word." *Smithsonian* 11: 10 (January 1981): 80-85.

Virginia L. Martin. "A Ninety-year Run. Giesen's: Costumers to St. Paul's Festivals and Families. 1872 - 1970," *Ramsey County History* 28:4 (Winter 1994): 4-15.

Jane McClure. "The St. Paul Curling Club and Its Colorful Century-old History," *Ramsey County History* 30:4 (Winter 1996): 4-14.

Larry Millett. "Lake Phalen palace a fairy tale come true," *St. Paul Pioneer Press Dispatch* (February 25, 1986): B2.

Bill Nye. "Bill Nye's Views," *St. Paul Daily Globe* (February 8, 1886): 1.

Bob Olsen. "Architect to the Kings of Carnival. 'Cap Wigington' and his Ice Palace 'Babies'," *Ramsey County History* 34: 4 (Spring 2000): 12-15.

Virginia L. Rahm. "The Nushka Club," *Minnesota History* 43 (Winter 1973): 303-307.

Rich Sharp. "Vulcans Don't Shed their Red after Carnival," *St. Paul Skyway News* (January 27, 1988): 34, 5.

Terry Spohn. "Raiders of the Lost Medallion," *Evergreen* 4:3 (March 9, 1982): 1, 3.

Jean E. Spraker. "The Rollicking Realm of Boreas. A Century of Carnivals in St. Paul," *Minnesota History* 49:8 (Winter 1985): 322-331.

Jason Tanz. "Lost Weekend: F. Scott and Budd Go to Dartmouth," *The New York Times* (February 7, 2003): D1, 7.

Jack Weinberg. "When Vulcan Chokes," *St. Paul Pioneer Press*, Pictorial Magazine (February 1, 1953): 1, 8, 12.

Susan E. Williams. "A Wild Hurrah: The Great Northern Celebration of 1893," *Minnesota History* 48: 3 (Fall 1982): 119-123.

Walter A. Williams. "Let's Go to South St. Paul. The Home of the Hook-'Em-Cows," *Western Magazine* XVI: 2 (August 1920): 78-79.

_____. "The St. Paul Ice Palace," *Harper's Weekly* XXX: 1522 (February 20, 1886): 119, 120.

_____. "Minnesota. The Winter Carnival at St. Paul. Laying the Cornerstone of the Ice Palace, January 3rd," *Frank Leslie's Illustrated Newspaper* LXIII: 1635 (January 15, 1887): 373, 375.

_____. "Minnesota. The Ice Palace at St. Paul, Formally Opened January 25th," *Frank Leslie's Illustrated Newspaper* LXV: 1689 (January 28, 1888): 397, 398.

_____. "St. Paul's Great Winter Sports Carnival," *Collier's* (February 26, 1916): 17.

_____."Revolt in the Northwest…" *Fortune* 13 (April 1936):117-119, 178, 183-184, 186, 190, 193-194, 197; and "Addendum," *Fortune* 14 (July 1936): 86-88, 142.

_____."Hook 'Em Cows," *Time* (February 8, 1937): 48.

_____."Ice Box Mardi Gras Warms Minnesotans," *Business Week* (February 12, 1966): 33.

_____."Keeping Your Guard Up," *St. Paul Pioneer Press*, Sunday Pictorial Magazine (January 28, 1968): 20.

Winter Carnival Official Publications

J. H. Hanson. *Ice Palace & Winter Carnival Souvenir*. St. Paul, MN: St. Paul Ice Palace & Winter Carnival Association (1885).

_____. *The Deluxe Souvenir View Book*. St. Paul, MN: Carnival Publishing Company (1916).

_____. *Official Souvenier (sic) Program*. St. Paul, MN: Webb Printing Company (1916).

_____. *Official Souvenir View Book*. St. Paul, MN: Carnival Publishing Company (1917).

_____. *75th Anniversary of the Fun-Filled St. Paul Winter Carnival, 1886-1961*. St. Paul, MN: St. Paul Winter Carnival Association (1961).

_____. *St. Paul Winter Carnival, 1886-1976. Commemorative Program honoring United States 200th Birthday*. St. Paul, MN: St. Paul Winter Carnival Association (1976).

Jerome Bette and Carol Morgan. *St. Paul Winter Carnival. 1886-1986 Official Centennial Calendar*. Minneapolis, MN: Carol Morgan Associates (1986).

Judith Yates Borger. *St. Paul Winter Carnival 100th Anniversary History*, 1886-1986. St. Paul, MN: St. Paul Winter Carnival Association (1986).

Index